FLAVORS FOR A CROWD

FLAVORS FOR A CROWD

PRACTICAL, LARGE QUANTITY RECIPES

JUDY L. HALPENNY

FIRST EDITION

Balboa Press books may be ordered through booksellers or by contacting:

Balboa Press
A Division of Hay House
1663 Liberty Drive
Bloomington, IN 47403
www.balboapress.com
1-(877) 407-4847

Pg. 237, Image by Emma Point

ISBN: 978-1-4525-4809-8 (e)
ISBN: 978-1-4525-4810-4 (sc)
ISBN: 978-1-4525-4811-1 (hc)

Library of Congress Control Number: 2012906953

Printed in the United States of America

Balboa Press rev. date: 5/7/2012

To all those who believed in me.

CONTENTS

PREFACE

▩ After several attempts at being a tree planter, I decided that even though I loved the people and the camp lifestyle, I was not cut out to be a tree planter … as was quite evident from my paychecks. So that's when my boyfriend (now husband) suggested that I apply for a job as a camp chef. I thought this was a great idea, even though I had no real experience as a cook and quite frankly was scared to death by the thought of people eating my food! I began as an assistant, and then moved on to be camp cook, first for small camps of fifteen and eventually cooking for large camps of seventy. When I started, I found that standard cookbook recipes were little help, geared as they were to feed four to six people. Simply scaling up by multiplying the measures seldom worked, especially with baking. Over the years I developed my own recipes, by intuition and luck as much as by science, to create dishes that were as mouthwatering and satisfying for a crowd as for an intimate dinner. So, here I am, after seven long seasons as a camp cook to writing a cookbook to pass on what I have learned to others faced with a similar challenge.

Cooking for large crowds can be as fun as it is daunting. There is a fine balance between keeping the camp happy and staying on budget. As a total self-made foodie, the hardest barrier for me to overcome when cooking for a large crowd is using compromising ingredients for the sake of the budget. There are many things that a camp cook has to buy, such as spices, baking ingredients, meat and special diet products, which can consume a large portion of the budget, which is not always a generous amount. At home, I would never use margarine, but when making cookies for a crowd of 70 the cost of butter would be insane!

Nutrition plays a very integral part of any meal and is especially important for those working incredibly physically long hours. Yet, it often goes unnoticed, as I have seen from my experiences of other forestry camps.

I put a lot of consideration into my meal planning and creation of meals, which probably has something to do with my perfectionist traits. If I wouldn't eat it myself, then why would I expect anyone else to eat it?

The purpose for me in writing this book is to share with the world my love & joy of cooking. I hope you have as much fun in cooking, sharing and eating these recipes as I have had creating them.

INTRODUCTION

▩ Over the years as a tree-planting cook I have had the joy to create what people told me were masterpiece meals on a budget, as well as some... not so great masterpieces. It is truly amazing what one can create with the ingredients on hand as long as there is one cup of willingness to experiment and two cups of trusting your instincts.

When cooking for large crowds keep in mind that everything from prepping vegetables to cooking times, needs to be extended. I always try to have everything ready 20 minutes before service or have a large pot of soup on hand so you can keep those hungry stomachs at bay. Also note that the recipes in this book have been doubled and tripled in accordance to what I would normally cook for a camp from 12 to 30 to 60, and certain items such as yeast breads have been measured through tested recipes, not necessarily by just doubling the recipe.

As camp chef, I have learned to cook for many different types of food allergies, such as celiac, as well as vegans and vegetarians. Some could say learning to cook with limited budgets and equipment in the middle of nowhere is the school of hard knocks and shapes one to become a really good cook. As a "bush cook" one has to learn to make do with what you have on hand, and there is no running to town in the middle of day when you are 40 miles away from the nearest town.

My inspiration for the title of this book "Flavors for a Crowd" was created because I love how flavors merge together from beginning to end. Tasting the different stages of flavor as a spaghetti sauce simmers or a soup bubbles brings me great joy. I owe a great debt of gratitude to all those who have tasted and raved about my food in my many different camps. If not for you, I may have never had the courage to write this book. Let the flavors merge!

MENU PLANS & THEME NIGHTS

▩ Deciding what to eat can depend on what is in season, the occasion, the weather, the age group you are cooking for, the tastes and preferences of the guests, as well as the budget. Included in the meal plans below are appetizers, bread, a soup, a salad, a main (vegetarian/meat) dish, a side dish, and a dessert. The meal plans are meant to be a simple guideline that will please any crowd. Below you will find an assortment of themes ranging from ethnic foods to simple one pot wonders.

Mexican Night

Salad

- Vegetarian Cobb Salad

Soup

- Mexican Bean Soup

Appetizers

- Corn Chips
- Guacamole
- Salsa
- or 7 Layer Dip

Bread

- Cornbread with Jalapenos & Sweet Corn

Main Dish

- Beef Tacos
- Or Chicken Fajitas
- Or Salsa & Cheese Chicken

Side Dishes

- Refried Beans
- Mexican Rice
- Grilled Corn on the Cob

Dessert

- Chocolate Zucchini Cake

Greek Night

Bread

- Pita

Soup

- Minestrone or Borscht

Appetizers

- Hummus
- Baba Gannuj
- Tzatziki
- Sundried Tomato & Fennel Spanakopitas

Salad

- Traditional Greek Salad or Mediterranean Orzo Salad

Main Dish

- Chicken or Pork Souvlaki
- Moussaka

Side Dishes

- Lemon Rice or Greek Roasted Potatoes

Dessert

- Apple or Berry Crisp

East Indian Night

Soup

- Curried Butternut Squash

Appetizers

- Pakoras or Samosas
- Papadums

Bread

- Naan

Salad

- Citrus Asian Salad

Main

- Butter Chicken
- Butter Paneer or Mattar Paneer

Side Dishes

- Curried Chickpeas with Green Peppers and Onions
- Red Lentil Dhal
- Rice Pulao

Dessert

- Strawberry Shortcake

Thai Night

Soup

- Tom Yum

Salad

- Vermicelli Noodle Salad with Peanut Sauce

Appetizer

- Thai Salad Rolls with Hoisan Sauce

Main

- Chicken/Vegetarian Green Curry with Mango Salsa

Side Dishes

- Pad Thai
- Sautéed Bok Choy with Pineapple & Oyster Sauce
- Jasmine Rice

Dessert

- Carrot Cake with Cream Cheese Icing

Italian Night

Soup

- Minestrone

Bread

- Garlic Bread

Appetizer

- Vegan Mushroom Pate & Crackers

Salad

- Roasted Garlic Caesar

Main

- Lasagna, Spaghetti or Parmesan Chicken

Side Dishes

- Sautéed Broccoli with Balsamic

Dessert

- Blueberry Cheesecake

SHOPPING LIST FOR A CROWD

■ The following ingredients list is a basic guideline for anyone needing to cook for a large crowd or camp and has been broken down into categories such as baking supplies or condiments. It is meant to serve as a starting point for having the right amount of ingredients on hand. When menu planning and ordering food from distributors, to stay on budget only order the ingredients you plan to use in the first rotation of meals. So, for example, if your meal plan does not include anything with cream cheese, then don't order or buy it until you need it. The amounts for each item were taken from my experience as cook for a 60 person camp, and these supplies would typically last four days.

Baking Supplies:

Brown Sugar – 20 kg

White Sugar – 20 kg

Icing Sugar – 4 x 1kg

Cocoa – 1 x 500 g

White Flour – 20 kg

Whole Wheat Flour – 20 kg

Baking Powder – 1 x 1 kg

Baking Soda – 2 x 500 g

Non-hydrogenated Canola Oil – 16 L

Non-hydrogenated Margarine – 15 kg

Instant Yeast – 1kg

Spray Pan Coating – 2 x 14 oz

Quick Cooking Oats – 10 kg

Coconut – 2 lbs

Raisins – 1 kg

Peanuts – 2.5 kg

Walnuts – 2 lbs

Sunflower Seeds – 2.5 kg

Lemon Juice - 500 ml

Vanilla – 1 L

Choc Chips – 10 kg

Rice Krispies - 1 case

Marshmallows – 2 x 400 g

Pancake Mix – 10 kg

Graham Crumbs – 4 x 500 g

Corn Meal – 1 kg

Corn Syrup – 2 x 1 kg

Frozen Pie Shells – 10

Olive Oil – 1.5 kg

Powdered Milk - 1 x 2.5 kg

Almonds – 1 kg

Wheat Bran – 1 kg

Molasses – 1 kg

Dried Pasta, Grains and Breads:

White Rice – 10 kg
Brown Rice – 10 kg
Spaghetti – 2.5 lbs
Lasagna Noodles – 2.5 lbs
Fettuccini – 2.5 lbs
Penne – 2.5 lbs
Barley – 1 x 500 g
Red River Cereal – 2 x 1 kg
Assorted Cereals -8 x 1 kg
Wraps – 12 dozen
Whole Wheat Bread – 15 loaves
Assorted Artisan Breads – 7 loaves

Condiments:

Mayonnaise – 4 L
Apple Cider Vinegar – 1 L
Balsamic Vinegar – 1 L
Ketchup – 2 x 2.85 L
Salsa 2 x4 L
BBQ Sauce – 2 L
Soya Sauce – 1 L
Yellow Mustard – 1 L
Flavored Mustards – 4 x 500 g
Relish – 500 g
Dill Pickles – 4 L
Banana Peppers – 4 L
Dijon Mustard – 500 ml
Pancake Syrup – 4 L
Hot Sauce – 1 L kg
Maple Syrup – 1 kg
Worcestershire Sauce – 1 kg
Sundried Tomatoes – 1 kg

Spices:

Basil
Oregano
Bay Leaves
Chili Powder
Crushed Chilies
Chives
Cinnamon
Dill
Garlic Powder
Garlic Salt
Salt
Peppercorns
Ginger
Mustard
Paprika
Parsley
Thyme
Cumin
Coriander
Nutmeg
Sage
Allspice
Taco Seasoning
Rosemary
Sesame seeds
Poppy seeds
Sprinkles
Montreal Steak Seasoning
Mrs. Dash
A. Vogel Herbamare Original Seasoning

Canned Goods:

Crushed Tomatoes – 6 x 2.4 L

Tuna – 2 x 1 kg

Canned Olives – 6 240 ml cans

Baked Beans (vegetarian) – 3 x 2.4 kg

Chick Peas – 2 x 2.4 L

Peanut Butter – 4 kg

Jam (assorted varieties) – 4 kg

Chicken Stock – 1 kg

Beef Stock – 1 kg

Vegetarian Stock – 1 kg

Dairy:

Milk – 8 x 4 L

Cream – 4 x 1 L

Whipping Cream – 2 x 1 L

Sour Cream – 2 L

Feta - 1 kg

Yogurt – 4 kg assorted flavors

Cream Cheese – 1.5 kg

Eggs – 45 dozen

Powdered Milk – 2.4 kg

Parmesan – 1 kg

Assorted Cheese – 5 kg

Meat:

Bacon – 3 x 5 kg

Breakfast Sausage – 2 x 5 kg

Lean Ground Beef – 6 x 5 kg

Chicken Thighs – 3 x 5 kg

Diced Beef – 2 x 5 kg

Boneless/Skinless Chicken Breasts – 3x 5 kg

Veggies:

Green Onions – 6 bunches

Broccoli - 1 case

Yellow Onions – 10 lbs.

Carrots – 10 lbs.

Zucchini – 2 lbs.

Mushrooms – 1 case

Green peppers – 2.5 kg

Red peppers – 1 kg

Celery – 2 lbs.

Potatoes – 1 case (100 potatoes)

Tomato – 24

Cucumber – 12

Eggplant – 5

Romaine – 1 case (24 heads)

Asparagus – 5 lbs.

Spinach – 1 x 2.4 kg bag

Peeled Garlic – 1 kg

Frozen Peas – 2 x 2 kg

Frozen Corn – 1 x 1 kg

Green Beans – 1 kg

Fruits:

Apples – 2 cases (approximately 54 apples in a case)

Oranges – 1 case

Bananas – 1 case

Frozen Berries – 1 kg

Grapes – 2 kg

Melons – 6

Cantaloupe – 6

Vegetarian/Vegan Items:

Soy Milk – 4 x 1 L

Ground Round – 1kg

Tofu – 1 case

Nutritional Yeast – 1 kg

Tamari – 1 500 ml bottle

Gomashio – 1 small package

Brags All Purpose Liquid Soy Seasoning – 1kg

Average Quantities Consumed Per Person

- Pasta – 1½ cups of cooked noodles per person.
- Rice and other grains – ½ cup per person – ¼ cup dry.
- Bread – One loaf of bread has an average of 18-20 slices. Average 4 slices per person per day, not including breakfast items such as French Toast. One loaf of bread will feed approximately 10 people for French Toast.
- Meat – 1½ pieces for chicken breasts for men; women will eat approximately 1 chicken breast each. Figure 1 ½ kg per person if used sliced/diced in a main dish such as Fettuccini Alfredo.
- Lettuce – 1 cup of salad per person or 8-10 heads for approximately 30 people.
- Eggs – 2 per person per breakfast meal, or for a camp plan to buy 30 - 40 dozen every 4 days. This range will depend on how many of the planned meals require eggs.
- Fresh Cooked Veggies – 1 cup per person for sides such as sautéed broccoli.
- Frozen Cooked Veggies – ½ cup per person.
- Raw Veggies – ¼ cup per person or 6-7 Asparagus spears, 7-8 baby carrots or 1 medium or ½ piece of a large cob of corn broken in half.
- Potatoes – 1 medium potato or 1 large Baker's potato cut in half.

EQUIPMENT LIST FOR A CROWD

▩ The following list is intended to be a guideline for the necessary equipment one might need when cooking for larger groups, whether in a camp or for catering purposes. You may include more or less of something according to your preferences and needs.

Essential Big Items:

- 2 100 cup coffee makers (1 for hot water)
- food processor
- hand held electric cake mixer
- hand blender
- industrial mix master
- 3 large mixing bowls
- 2 medium mixing bowls
- 3 small mixing bowls
- 1 large colander
- 2 x 8 inch deep hotel pans
- 3 x 4 inch medium deep hotel pans
- 4 x 1-2 inch deep hotel pans
- 2-3 hotel pan lids
- 3 large cookie sheets
- 2 medium cookie sheets
- 2 small cookie sheets
- 2 square cake pans
- 1 large roasting pan
- 2 large pots
- 2 medium pots
- 2-3 very small pots
- 1 large rondeau; useful for roasts, roasting veggies, cooking sauces
- 2 large frying pans and 1 small frying pan
- 5 bread pans
- 3 pie plates
- 1 large cutting board/2 small cutting boards
- 1 large industrial 24 muffin tin

Essential Small Things:

- 3 large wooden spoons
- 2 small wooden spoons
- 3 tongs
- 2 ladles
- 1 pastry brush
- 3 solid metal spoons
- 2 slotted metal spoons
- 1 eight cup measuring cup
- 2 four cup measuring cups
- 1 two cup measuring cup
- 2 metal flipper
- 2 plastic flippers
- 1 oven thermometer
- fridge & freezer thermometers
- 1 meat thermometer
- 1 good quality vegetable peeler
- 1 good quality can opener
- 1 large funnel
- 1 small funnel
- 1 cheese grater
- 1 large potato masher
- 1 large rolling pin
- 1 large whisk
- 1 small whisk
- scissors
- 1 measuring spoon set
- 2 pie servers
- 3 good quality chef knives
- 1 good quality serrated knife
- 2 BBQ lighters
- 2 plastic spatulas
- 1 grill scraper for grill

TIPS FOR COOKING FOR A CROWD

▪ Here are a few tips that I have found helpful in my many seasons of cooking in camps.

- Muffin tins are useful to poach eggs in when cooking Eggs Benny dishes. Make sure to spray the muffin tins really well!
- Use parchment paper as much as possible as it will save you time in having to wash and scrub dishes.
- Cook rice in a deep hotel pan and in the oven rather than over the stove. Turns out perfectly every time.
- Tray out bacon on parchment paper, then roll and place in a bus bin. This will save you time in the early morning when cooking breakfast.
- Break fresh ginger into pieces and store in the freezer. Just before using, pull desired amount from freezer; it will be easier to cut and you will always have ginger on hand.
- When buying coconut milk look for brands that have coconut listed as the first ingredient, not water, and that have a coconut percentage of 50% or higher. The higher the percentage of coconut the more flavor your dish will have.
- When buying meats, try to avoid buying IQF (Individually Quick Frozen) products, they are filled with hormones and will shrink considerably when cooking.
- When cooking rice, the amount varies depending on whether the recipe is a side dish or main course. For a side dish, I use a ¼ cup per person and for a main dish such as Jambalaya; I use ½ a cup per person. When cooking large quantities (12 servings or more) I use a large hotel pan to cook the rice and I cook it in the oven at 400°F.
- When cooking dishes such as rice or casseroles, instead of using a metal hotel lid cover with plastic wrap and tinfoil. This will prevent the dish from drying out and will seal in moisture. As long as the plastic wrap is covered with tinfoil, it will not melt into the food. Important: Must be used together, tinfoil used alone will leave tinfoil spots and plastic wrap will melt.
- Refrigerate cookie dough prior to rolling out cookies. This will make it much easier to tray out the cookie dough. Rather than making individual cookies, tray the dough onto a large cookie sheet and cut the squares into desired sizes after baking.

- Oil hands before kneading bread dough. It will much be much easier to knead dough with oiled hands.
- Use an ice cream scoop to scoop muffin mix into the muffin tins.
- Place a piece of apple in brown sugar to prevent the sugar from lumping and hardening.
- If you burn a pan, simply place baking soda or salt to cover the bottom of the pot and cover with a thin layer of water, then boil until all the liquid is gone. You will be able scrape any burnt pieces off.
- Add a drop of cold water to any egg white; this will help the egg stiffen faster.
- Use scissors to cut the ends off green beans.
- Rub your hands on a stainless steel sink to help get rid of any garlic or onion smells.
- To release the bitterness from a cucumber, simply cut the top off and rub the top of the cucumber on the longer portion and the bitterness, a white substance will be brought to the top. Rinse before using.
- Always salt your pasta water to help your pasta cook properly.
- Rinse pasta under cold water for pasta salads and add a touch of olive oil to prevent the noodles from sticking.
- Pasta is finished when the edges of the pasta turn white. And throwing that spaghetti noodle at the wall to see if it sticks to test doneness really does work!
- When storing leftover tofu place in a Ziploc container with water and it will generally keep for up to five days or more.
- If veggies have gone limp, try soaking them in cold water to zap them back into shape.
- If you ever need to quickly cool something such as pasta noodles, cake or dessert, simply place it in the freezer for 15 minutes. But don't forget about it!
- If your dish has turned out too salty add a couple of potatoes to the dish. This should soak up some of the excess salt.
- Use leftover egg cartons for quickly cooling dishes. Place hot dish on top of egg carton and cool at room temperature, stirring often, and place in fridge immediately.

PROTEINS FOR VEGETARIANS & VEGANS

▩ When cooking for vegetarians and vegans it is important to have a protein in their meal. I would often use meat recipes but substitute a vegetarian protein for the meat. There is a wide selection of vegetarian proteins readily available.

Some of these are:

- Any beans (legumes) such as black beans, soybeans, fava beans and chick peas (also known as garbanzo beans).
- Other legumes such as peas, lentils and peanuts.
- Ground soy meat, known as ground round, which is available in the flavors Mexican, Italian or original.
- Tempeh is a product, found at most health food stores, that is made from fermented soy. A very tasty addition to any meal. Can be grilled on its own or add a few dashes of Bragg's or Tamari and add to any stir fry.
- Textured Vegetarian Protein (TVP); the best brand I have found is Bob's Red Mill TVP. Simply add hot water to TVP and let sit for 15 minutes before adding it to any dish.
- For Mexican dishes, refried beans or pureed black beans are a great component to any Mexican vegetarian dish. (When using refried beans out of a can I use a hand blender to give the beans a smoother consistency.)
- Nuts such as almonds can be used, although use in moderation as they have a very high carb index.
- Seeds such as pumpkin, sesame, hemp and sunflower seeds.
- And of course tofu... such a versatile product. I found when adding tofu to sauces that it is best to grill or sauté first. You can even add it to baked goods ... and no one will ever know.
- Leafy green vegetables – Yes! They have protein, in some cases just as much as any meat source. There are so many to choose from: kale, spinach, parsley, green leaf lettuce, red leaf lettuce, the list is endless.
- Nutritional Yeast – Deactivated yeast that is full of protein and B vitamins. Sprinkle on popcorn, tofu, kale or add to dips.

BREAKFAST

Muesli

Loved by all and a great way to use up any leftover fruits.

12 servings	32 servings	60 servings	Ingredients
6 cups	15 cups	30 cups	Instant Oats
3 cups	7 ½ cups	15 cups	Soy Milk/Cream/ Milk
1 ½ cups	3 ¾ cups	7 ½ cups	Orange Juice
1 ½ cups	3 ¾ cups	7 ½ cups	Shredded Apples
¾ cup	1 ½ cups	2 ½ cups	Dried Cranberries
¾ cups	2 cups	4 cups	Bananas
¾ cups	2 cups	4 cups	Watermelon
¾ cups	2 cups	4 cups	Cantaloupe
6 cups	15 cups	30 cups	Coconut
¾ cups	2 cups	4 cups	Grapes
1 Tbsp;	3 Tbsp	5 Tbsp	Vanilla
¾ cup	2 cups	4 cups	Maple Syrup/Agave Syrup/Honey

Directions:

- Mix oats with cream, milk and orange juice.
- Shred apples, dice watermelon, cantaloupe and slice grapes. Add bananas to the mixture just before serving. You can use any leftover fruit. Oranges are great too!
- Toss with vanilla.
- Add fruit mixture to oat mixture, then add coconut, dried cranberries and sweetener. Use whole sweeteners such as honey, maple syrup or agave syrup.
- Add more cream or soy milk if mixture is too dry. Let mixture sit overnight so the oats can absorb all the liquid.
- Will keep for up to 4 days in the fridge.

Good Old Fashioned Pancakes

A fail proof recipe that I have used over the years. Make sure to use fresh baking powder so you don't end up with a dud.

12 Servings	32 Servings	60 servings	Ingredients
4 ½ cups	12 cups	22 ½ cups	All-purpose flour
3 Tbsp	7 Tbsp	12 Tbsp	Baking powder
2 tsp	11/2 Tbsp	3 Tbsp	Salt
3 Tbsp	3/4 cup	1 1/4 cups	Sugar/Honey
3 ¾ cups	9 cups	18 ¾ cups	Milk
3	7	15	Eggs
3 Tbsp	7 Tbsp	1 cup	Oil or melted Butter
1 Tbsp	3 Tbsp	5 Tbsp	Vanilla

Directions:

- In a large bowl, mix together the flour, baking powder, salt and sugar. Make a well in the center and pour in the milk, add the eggs and melted butter. Mix until all ingredients are mixed together but don't over mix. It is okay if there are a few lumps in the batter; they will disappear as the pancakes cook.
- Heat a lightly oiled griddle or frying pan over medium high heat. Pour approximately ¼ cup of mix for each pancake. Brown pancakes on both sides.
- Serve with blueberry or raspberry purée, maple syrup, whipped cream, sliced bananas or stewed strawberries.

Blueberry Pancakes

Makes you go mmm…

12 Servings	32 Servings	60 Servings	Ingredients
4 ½ cups	12 cups	22 ½ cups	All-purpose flour
2 tsp	11/2 Tbsp	3 Tbsp	Salt
3 Tbsp	7 Tbsp	12 Tbsp	Baking powder
3 Tbsp	3/4 cup	1 1/4 cups	Sugar
3 ¾ cups	9 cups	18 ¾ cups	Milk
3	8	15	Eggs
3 Tbsp	7 Tbsp	1 cup	Oil or melted butter
1 Tbsp	2 ½ Tbsp	5 Tbsp	Vanilla
1 ½ cups	3 ¾ cups	7 ½ cups	Blueberries (frozen)

Directions:

- In a large bowl, sift together the flour, baking powder, salt and sugar. Make a well in the center and pour in the milk, add the eggs and melted butter or oil; fold in fold in frozen blueberries and mix until smooth.
- Heat a lightly oiled griddle or frying pan over medium high heat. Pour approximately ¼ cup of mix for each pancake. Brown on both sides.
- Serve right away or keep warm in oven at a low temperature. Place parchment in between each layer of pancakes to prevent them from sticking together.

Pancake Variations:

- ***Apple Cinnamon*** – Substitute blueberries with shredded red apples and heaps of cinnamon.
- ***Chocolate Chip Walnut*** – Add walnuts and chocolate chips right before you are about to cook the pancakes on a hot griddle.
- ***Cranberry and White Chocolate Chips*** – Add dried cranberries and chunks of white chocolate.
- ***12 Grain*** – Substitute white flour with a blend of whole wheat and whole grain flour
- ***Banana*** – Add ripened banana to your pancake mixture. Mash the bananas with a potato masher first before adding to batter.
- ***Banana, Chocolate Chip & Walnut*** – Add all three together for a lovely flavor.

Peppercorn Maple Bacon

Here is a nice twist on plain old bacon.

12 Servings	32 Servings	60 Servings	Ingredients
36 Slices	96	180	Bacon
Drizzled over top			Maple Syrup
Ground over top			Fresh ground Pepper

Directions:

- Preheat oven to 325°F.
- When cooking bacon for large quantities I layer the bacon on a large cookie sheet with the fat side of the bacon facing up.
- Before cooking the bacon, drizzle maple syrup over and grind fresh peppercorns over top.
- Make sure to watch the bacon as the syrup will burn easily.
- Cook bacon for about 55 minutes (will vary depending on your oven and whether you are using a convection oven). Make sure to mix the bacon around at least once with tongs.

Mexican Style Egg Burritos

Packed full of protein, these burritos will make anyone smile at 6 a.m.!

12 Servings	32 Servings	60 Servings	Ingredients
30	80	150	Eggs
1 ½ cups	4 cups	7 ½ cups	Onions
1 ½ cups	4 cups	7 ½ cups	Red Pepper
1 ½ cups	4 cups	7 ½ cups	Green Pepper
1 ½ cups	4 cups	7 ½ cups	Black Beans
1 ½ cups	4 cups	7 ½ cups	Salsa
1 ½ cups	4 cups	7 ½ cups	Cheddar Cheese
1 ½ tsp	4 tsp	7 ½ tsp	Pepper
1 ½ Tbsp	3 Tbsp	8 Tbsp	Chicken/Vegetable Oxo
1 cup	3 cups	5 cups	Water or milk
12	30	60	Whole Wheat Tortillas

Optional: Fresh Cilantro

Directions:

- Preheat oven to 400°F.
- Dice onions, green pepper and red pepper. Heat oil on grill. Sauté onions until brown, add green and red peppers. Set aside.
- Drain black beans, rinse and set aside.
- Wash and mince cilantro.
- Whisk eggs, water or milk and chicken stock together. Use vegetarian stock if cooking for vegetarians or vegans. Tip: Rather than milk, water helps to create light, fluffy eggs.
- There are two ways to cook scrambled eggs in large quantities: Method One: Spray large hotel pan with non-stick Pam. Place whisked eggs in insert and cook until a light, fluff y consistency has been achieved. Stir with whisk every so often. Method Two: On medium heat, heat oiled grill and slowly pour egg mixture onto grill and, using the back of a spatula, scramble the eggs by pulling the egg mixture towards you and then away from you.

- Once eggs are cooked, mix beans, cilantro, salsa, onions and peppers into egg mixture.
- Scoop two ladles of egg mixture onto 6 inch tortilla shells. Add a dollop of sour cream.
- Fold the side of the tortilla shell closest to you over the mixture, fold the sides in and roll the wrap away from you until you have reached the other end.
- Serve with Hashbrowns.

Eggs Benny Two Ways

A few simple ingredients that lend a hand to a quick and easy breakfast item to go. If using hollandaise sauce, I buy a premade mix which is simple and quick.

12 Servings	32 Servings	60 Servings	Ingredients
18	45	90	Eggs
18	45	90	English Muffins
18	45	90	Real Cheddar Cheese Slices and Tomato Slices
18	45	90	Slices of ham and ¼ Cup each Hollandaise Sauce

Directions:

- Preheat oven to 375°F.
- Spray muffin tins with non-stick Pam. Crack eggs into muffin tins and cook for 45 minutes. For a different flavor add ham to the bottom of each individual muffin tin, which also helps to prevent sticking.
- Line English muffins onto cookie sheet; place eggs from muffin tray onto English muffin and top with hollandaise sauce.
- Or place sliced tomato and cheddar cheese slices on top of egg and muffin and bake in oven over medium low heat until the cheese has melted.

Scrambled Eggs with Chipotle Peppers & Cream Cheese

This dish has a nice smoky flavor and if you really like heat, add more peppers.

12 Servings	32 Servings	60 Servings	Ingredients
24	64	120	Eggs
1 ½ cups	4 cups	7 ½ cups	Green onion
1 ½ cup	4 cups	7 ½ cups	Red pepper
1 ½ cup	4 cups	7 ½ cups	Brown Mushrooms
1 ½ tsp	1 Tbsp	3 Tbsp	Chipotle Peppers (Canned)
6 Tbsp	1 cup	2 cups	Cream Cheese
1 ½ Tbsp	3 Tbsp	8 Tbsp	Chicken Stock
1 cup	3 cups	5 cups	Milk or water
1 ½ tsp	1 Tbsp	2 Tbsp	Sea Salt & Pepper

Directions:

- Wash and dice peppers and green onions. Wash mushrooms really well and slice into halves.
- Mix eggs with cream cheese and water or milk. Add salt, pepper and stock.
- Whisk until light bubbles form and cream cheese is well blended.
- Deseed the chipotle peppers. I recommend wearing gloves as the membranes of chipotle peppers are very hot.
- Dice the chipotle peppers into very fine pieces. Add to egg mixture.
- Preheat oiled grill to medium heat and sauté peppers and onions and set aside once onions are soft. Add eggs to grill and using the back of the spatula lightly pull the eggs towards you, turning ever so slightly until the eggs are scrambled.
- Once eggs are cooked add sauteed peppers and onions. For large quantities it is best to cook in batches.

Mexican Scrambled Tofu

Such a scrumptious alternative for vegans.... I can`t believe it`s not scrambled eggs!

12 Servings	32 Servings	60 Servings	Ingredients
1 ½ Blocks	4 Blocks	7 Blocks	Firm Tofu
6 sprigs	12 Sprigs	15 Sprigs	Diced Green Onions
2	4	6	Diced Avocados
3	8	15	Diced Tomatoes
¾ Cup	2 Cups	5 Cups	Black Beans
6 Tbsp	12 Tbsp	1 Cup	Olive Oil
½ Tbsp	1 Tbsp	2 Tbsp	Sea Salt
1 Cup	3 Cups	5 Cups	Salsa
1 Tbsp	3 Tbsp	5 Tbsp	Oregano
1 Tbsp	2 Tbsp	4 Tbsp	Cumin

Directions:

- Using your hands, crumble tofu apart.
- Dice green onions, avocado, and tomato.
- Heat oil in a frying pan over medium low and sauté green onions and tofu until onions are soft.
- Add sea salt, salsa, oregano and cumin.
- Drain and rinse black beans and add to mixture.
- Just before serving add diced tomatoes and avocado to the pan and mix into the tofu.
- Serve with miso soup and toast.

BLT's

A quick-to-serve breakfast item that doesn't require a plate and tastes delicious!

12 Servings	32 Servings	60 Servings	Ingredients
12	30	60	12 Grain/Whole wheat Bagels
½ cup	1 cup	2 cups	Mayonnaise
24	60	120	Bacon Slices
½ Head	1 ½ Heads	3 Heads	Lettuce
3	8	12	Tomatoes

Directions:

- Preheat oven to 375°F and cook bacon for 45 minutes or use leftover bacon. Drain off grease and let bacon cool.
- Wash and slice tomatoes and lettuce.
- Slice bagels in half and spread bagels on a large hotel sheet or baking sheet. On low heat toast bagels for a couple of minutes, spread mayo on both sides and add tomato, lettuce and bacon. Keep them warm in the oven for only a few minutes as the lettuce will get soggy. Best to serve right away.

Scrambled Eggs with Pesto, Feta, Cherry Tomatoes & Spinach

Use fresh homemade or store-bought pesto. Either way it will be delicious!

12 Servings	32 Servings	60 Servings	Ingredients
24	60	120	Eggs
¾ cups	2 cups	4 cups	Milk or Water
1 Tbsp	3 Tbsp	8 Tbsp	Chicken or Veggie Stock
½ Tbsp	2 Tbsp	3 Tbsp	Pepper
1 ½ cups	4 cups	7 ½ cups	Onions
6 cups	16 cups	30 cups	Spinach
½ cup	¾ cup	1 cup	Pesto
1 cup	3 cups	5 cups	Cherry Tomatoes
¾ cups	2 cups	3 ¾ cups	Feta

Directions:

- Crack eggs into a large bowl.
- Add water or milk and mix until yolks are slightly broken. You can also use a hand blender instead of a whisk.
- Add stock and pepper.
- Dice cherry tomatoes in half.
- Add oil to grill and heat to medium heat.
- Peel and dice onions into medium-sized cubes. Grill until soft and set aside.
- Slowly pour egg mixture onto hot grill, using the back of a spatula or metal flipper pull the eggs towards you and away from you until the eggs begin to coagulate. As the eggs begin to scramble gently lift eggs into the air with utensils, dropping them back onto the grill. This will help form fluffier eggs.
- When cooking for large quantities I usually scramble the eggs in batches and transfer them to a hotel pan. I then add the onions, pesto and feta and place in oven on low temperature until you I have cooked all the eggs.

Cheddar Cheese Egg Soufflé

Not your traditional soufflé but a camp-style soufflé that is sure to please.

12 Servings	32 Servings	60 Servings	Ingredients
33	90	180	Eggs
¾ cup	2 cups	3 ¾ cups	Heavy Cream
1 ½ Tbsp	3 Tbsp	5 Tbsp	Chicken/Vegetarian Stock
1 Tbsp	2 Tbsp	3 Tbsp	Pepper
1 ½ cups	4 cups	7 ½ cups	Cheddar Cheese
5 sprigs	8 sprigs	15 sprigs	Green Onions

Directions:

- Preheat oven to 400°F.
- Grate cheddar cheese.
- Wash and dice green onion.
- Beat eggs with cream, pepper and stock until yolks are broken.
- Add cheese and green onion to the egg mixture.
- Pour egg mixture into a greased medium-sized hotel pan.
- Cook covered for the first hour and then uncover for the last ½ hour or until a soft round top forms and turns brown.

French Toast

The more flavors you put into the egg mixture the better tasting your French toast will be. Don't be shy … why not try some bourbon.

12 Servings	32 Servings	60 Servings	Ingredients
24 slices	64 slices	120 slices	Thickly Sliced Whole Wheat Bread
12	32	60	Eggs
¾ cup	2 cups	3 ¾ cups	Milk
¾ tsp	2 tsp	3 ¾ tsp	Salt
1 Tbsp	3 Tbsp	5 Tbsp	Brown Sugar
1 Tbsp	3 Tbsp	5 Tbsp	Cinnamon
1 ½ tsp	2 Tbsp	3 Tbsp	Vanilla

Directions:

- In a large bowl, combine eggs, milk and salt.
- Add vanilla, brown sugar and cinnamon together.
- Whisk ingredients together until light and frothy.
- Heat grill and spray lightly with a non-stick spray or melt butter to coat grill.
- Lightly coat the bread by dipping into egg mixture (a couple of seconds on each side; otherwise it will become soggy) and grill on both sides until golden brown.
- Serve with whipped cream and stewed strawberries.

Frittata

This recipe is great for using leftover items such as hash browns and breakfast meats. If you have vegetarians, I make one dish for the veggies and one dish for the meat eaters.

12 Servings	32 Servings	60 Servings	Ingredients
6 cups	24 cups	45 cups	Left over Hash-browns/Or Frozen Hashbrowns
24	64	120	Eggs
1 Tbsp	3 Tbsp	5 Tbsp	Chicken/Vegetable Stock
½ Tbsp	1 Tbsp	2 Tbsp	Cracked pepper
2	3	4	Green peppers
2	3	4	Red Peppers
1 ½	2	3	Onions
2 ¼ cups	6 cups	11 ¼ cups	Cheddar Cheese

Left over breakfast meat (optional)

Directions:

- If using frozen hash browns, cook them first. Follow instructions on back of package. Toss with seasoning salt and Montreal steak seasoning to taste.
- Heat oven to 350°F.
- Dice peppers and onions into medium-sized chunks. Heat grill to medium heat. Lightly sauté peppers and onions. Put aside. Shred cheese into a bowl.
- Using a shallow hotel pan, grease bottom of hotel pan with Pam or cover with parchment paper. Place a layer of seasoned hash browns over the bottom. Spread a layer of peppers, onions and cheese.
- Combine eggs with pepper and chicken or vegetable stock and gently whisk until yolks are broken.
- Pour a thin layer of egg mixture over hash browns. Depending on the quantity you are making you may need to use an additional hotel pan. The frittata should reach no higher than one half of the insert.
- Bake uncovered for 1 hour or until golden brown on top

Grandma Bjorndal's Gourmet Crepes

This recipe is actually a family favorite. The only time I ever attempted to make this in camp it turned out to be a complete disaster as the cook shack was not level so the crepe batter ended up going towards the back of the grill, lesson learned - make sure your grill is level!

12 Servings	32 Servings	60 Servings	Ingredients
12 cups	30 cups	60 cups	Milk
15	40	75	Eggs
3 cups	8 cups	15 cups	Flour
1 ½ cups	4 cups	7 ½ cups	Brown sugar
2 Tbsp	5 Tbsp	10 Tbsp	Vanilla

Directions:

- Mix dry ingredients together. Add wet ingredients and mix until no lumps appear. Mixture should be runny, as crepes are meant to be thin.
- Heat griddle and melt butter, using a ladle or measuring cup with a spout pour mixture evenly in a circle. Cook each side until slightly browned.
- Serve with fruit compote, whip cream or sprinkle with icing sugar and maple syrup.

Mega Fruit Salad

Healthy and delicious...

12 Servings	32 Servings	60 Servings	Ingredients
1 ½ cups	4 cups	7 ½ cups	Apple
1 ½ cups	4 cups	7 ½ cups	Grape
1 ½ cups	4 cups	7 ½ cups	Orange
1 ½ cups	4 cups	7 ½ cups	Melon
1 ½ cups	4 cups	7 ½ cups	Pineapple
1 ½ cups	4 cups	7 ½ cups	Banana
¾ cups	2 cups	3 ¾ cups	Orange Juice
¾ cups	2 cups	3 ¾ cups	Dried Cranberries
¾ cup	2 cup	3 ¾ cups	Slivered Almonds
2 Tbsp	5 Tbsp	8 Tbsp	Vanilla
1 Tbsp	3 Tbsp	5 Tbsp	Lemon Juice

Directions:

- Peel and dice oranges, melon, pineapple into medium-sized chunks.
- Dice apples and peeled bananas and toss in lemon juice to prevent them from turning brown.
- Combine all fruit and toss in orange juice and vanilla.
- Add slivered almonds and dried cranberries just before serving.

Oatmeal

Quick and easy. Try different flavors like the ones listed below to mix it up.

12 Servings	32 Servings	60 Servings	Ingredients
4 ½ cups	12 cups	22 ½ cups	Instant Oatmeal
12 cups	32 cups	60 cups	Water
1 tsp	2 Tbsp	1 Tbsp	Salt

Directions:

- In a medium-sized commercial stock pot, bring water to boil.
- Once boiling, slowly add oatmeal and stir with a large whisk to prevent clumps from forming.
- Add additions to oatmeal.
- Stir constantly and cook for 5 minutes.
- Reheat leftover oatmeal by adding hot water and whisking until the oatmeal is nice and smooth.

Additions:

- Cinnamon, Raisons & Brown Sugar
- Brown Sugar & Chopped Walnuts
- Dried Cranberries & Brown Sugar
- Flax, Brown Sugar & Maple Syrup
- Frozen Blueberries or Raspberries & Brown Sugar

Hashbrowns

Use leftover baked potatoes, or if you are in a pinch substitute fresh potatoes for frozen hash browns and add the same seasonings as below.

12 Servings	32 Servings	60 Servings	Ingredients
18	48	90	Red or Bakers Potatoes
2	3	4	Yellow Onions or Green Onions
6 Tbsp	1 cup	1 ½ cups	Butter or non-hydrogenated margarine
1 Tbsp	3 Tbsp	5 Tbsp	Montreal Steak Seasoning or Mrs. Dash
to taste			Seasoning Salt
to taste			Sea Salt
to taste			Cracked Pepper

Directions:

- Cut potatoes into quarters (as you cut the potatoes, place in cold water to prevent them from turning grey) and boil in salted water until just about soft. Strain and refrigerate for later or set aside.
- Peel and dice onions and begin sautéing in melted butter over medium heat, adding potatoes and seasoning.
- Adjust seasoning to taste. Sauté potatoes until they are golden brown.
- Other additions include sautéed mushrooms or chives or leftover diced sweet potatoes.

BREADS

Basic Bread

This recipe uses regular yeast; you can substitute instant yeast which will cut down the rising time. See instant bread recipe below for directions.

12 Servings	32 Servings	60 Servings	Ingredients
2 Tbsp	5 Tbsp	10 Tbsp	Yeast
1 Tbsp	4 Tbsp	7 Tbsp	Sugar
3 ¾ cups	10 cups	18 ¾ cups	Warm Water
9 cups	24 cups	45 cups	All-purpose Flour
1 Tbsp	2 ½ Tbsp	5 Tbsp	Salt
3 Tbsp	8 Tbsp	15 Tbsp	Olive Oil

Directions:

- Measure yeast and half the sugar into the bottom of a medium-sized bowl. Slowly add lukewarm water. Water should be 105 – 110°F. The temperature of the water can be tested by using your elbow to see if it is tepid. The key thing to remember when making bread is the temperature of the water: too hot and it will kill the yeast; too cool and it will take a really long time to rise. If you are using instant yeast, however, water at a temperature of 130°F can be added to the flour and yeast. See instant yeast recipe.
- With a fork, quickly mix yeast, sugar and water together for a few seconds and wait for yeast to bubble to the surface. It will take approximately 10 minutes.
- Measure the remaining sugar and other dry ingredients into a large bowl and sift with your hands. Make a well in the center of the dry ingredients and add the yeast mixture to the well.
- With oiled hands, knead ingredients together for a few minutes and add olive oil. It is important that the flour and water mixture is kneaded prior to adding the oil in order to produce the gluten, otherwise it will make it tougher for the gluten to form. Continue kneading for about 10 minutes longer. You will know when the dough is kneaded enough when you notice the formation of air pockets in the dough.
- The dough should be wet enough that the dough kneads easily, however not so wet that it sticks to the sides of the bowl. If too wet, add a sprinkle of flour until the desired consistency is reached. If too dry, slowly add no more than a couple of tablespoons of water at a time.

- Once finished kneading, form a round ball and place plastic wrap over top. This will ensure that the dough will not dry out. Let stand for an hour and a half to two hours or until the dough has doubled in size. To help bread rise place near a warm oven or a sunny spot. Do not place dough near any drafts or cold areas; this will prevent the dough from rising properly.
- Once dough has doubled in size, knead it down again for another few minutes. If making more than one loaf, cut individual loaves into the size of a bread pan. Shape into loaves and place into loaf pan. Let rise again in the loaf pans for another hour or until the bread has doubled in size.
- Pre-heat oven to 375°F and lightly spread olive oil over the top of loaves just before baking. This will help create a nice, soft, chewy crust. For a crustier crust skip the oil and spray with water every 20 minutes or so.

Tip: Place a shallow pan of water in the oven to help bread form a nice crust and soft, chewy interior.

- Bake bread loaves for approximately 40 minutes or until browned on top. To test if bread is done, knock on the bottom of the loaf with your knuckles; if it sounds hollow then the bread is finished. Internal bread temperature should reach 195°F.

Instant Yeast Bread

Instant yeast recipes require less yeast to produce a loaf of bread.

12 Servings	32 Servings	60 Servings	Ingredients
1 ½ Tbsp	4 Tbsp	7 Tbsp	Instant Yeast
2 Tbsp	5 Tbsp	8 Tbsp	Sugar
3 ¾ cups	10 cups	18 ¾ cups	Warm Water
9 cups	24 cups	45 cups	All-purpose Flour
1 Tbsp	5 Tbsp	7 Tbsp	Sea Salt
3 Tbsp	8 Tbsp	15 Tbsp	Olive Oil

Directions:

- Preheat oven to 375°F.
- Measure the above dry ingredients, including the yeast, into a large bowl, sift with fingers and make a well in the center to add hot water. Instant yeast recipes can withstand a temperature of up to 130°F.
- With instant yeast it requires one less step of kneading and therefore only needs to rise once. Once all the ingredients have been measured into a medium-sized bowl, knead dough until air pockets have formed: about 10-15 minutes. The dough should be well oiled so it pulls easily away from the side of the bowl. Once you have finished kneading, cut dough into individual loaves and shape into sizeable pieces and place into a greased loaf pan.
- Cover the loaves and let the loaves rise in the loaf pans until they have doubled in size or about an hour and place in preheated oven. Bake for 40 minutes or so.
- To test if bread is done, knock on the bottom of the loaf with your knuckles; if it sounds hollow then the bread is finished. Internal bread temperature should reach 195°F.

Bread Additions:

The following additions make for great variations to that regular old bread loaf. Simply add ingredients to the dough after the wet and dry ingredients have been mixed.

- Sundried tomatoes & Asiago
- Diced garlic cloves & garlic powder

- Diced pitted black olives & Sundried tomatoes
- Italian herbs (oregano, basil, rosemary, thyme)
- Shredded cheddar cheese & black olives
- Parmesan cheese
- Green onion & shredded cheddar cheese
- Substitute whole wheat flour or 12 grain bread flour for a heartier, healthier loaf
- Substitute 1 cup of cooked Red River cereal or cooked oatmeal for 1 cup of white flour for a country grain loaf

Bread Toppings:

For a nice crust try brushing the top of your bread with the following:

- Cold water for a crisp crust
- Egg white and two teaspoons of water for a shiny crust
- Egg yolk and two teaspoons of water for a golden crust
- Milk for a soft crust
- Or coat with egg yolk and cold water and sprinkle with one of the following: coarse sea salt, garlic powder, grated cheese, minced garlic and sundried tomatoes, minced green onion, poppy seeds or sunflower seeds or fresh herbs such as rosemary.

Garlic Bread

Serve warm with spaghetti or lasagna. For a nutritious option, substitute1 cup of whole grain bread flour for 1 cup of white flour.

12 Servings	32 Servings	60 Servings	Ingredients
1 ½ Tbsp	4 Tbsp	7 Tbsp	Instant Yeast
2 Tbsp	5 Tbsp	8 Tbsp	Sugar
3 ¾ cups	10 cups	18 ¾ cups	Warm Water
9 cups	24 cups	45 cups	All-purpose Flour
1 Tbsp	5 Tbsp	7 Tbsp	Sea Salt
3 Tbsp	8 Tbsp	15 Tbsp	Olive Oil
1 ½ cups	5 cups	7 cups	Garlic Butter

Directions:

- Measure yeast and sugar into the bottom of a medium-sized bowl. Slowly add lukewarm water to yeast and sugar. Water should be 105 – 110°F.
- Quickly mix yeast, sugar and water together with a fork for a few seconds and wait for yeast to bubble to the surface. It will take approximately 10 minutes.
- Measure dry ingredients into a large bowl. Make a well in the center of the dry ingredients and add the yeast mixture to the well. With oiled hands, knead ingredients together for a few minutes and add olive oil. Keep kneading for about 10 minutes longer, until air pockets start to form in the bread dough.
- Mixture should be wet enough that the dough kneads easily, however not so wet that it sticks to the sides of the bowl. If too wet, add a sprinkle of flour until desired consistency is reached. If too dry, slowly add no more than a couple of tablespoons of water at a time.
- Once finished kneading, form a round ball and place plastic wrap over top. This will ensure that it will not dry out. Let stand for 1 ½ hours to two hours. Place dough by a warm oven and let bread double in size.
- Important: Do not place dough near any drafts or cold areas. This will prevent the dough from rising properly.
- Once dough has doubled in size, knead down again. If making more than one loaf, cut individual loaves to a bread pan. Knead again for a few minutes and place into loaf pan. Let rise again in the loaf pans for another hour.

- Pre-heat oven to 375°F and lightly spread olive oil over top of loaves just before cooking.
- Cook loaves for approximately 30 minutes or until browned on top. To test if bread is done, knock on the bottom of the loaf with your knuckles; if it sounds hollow then the bread is finished or check for an internal temperature of 190°F.
- Let bread cool and slice the loaves lengthwise, then spread garlic butter evenly on each side. Toast bread in oven at 350°F for about 20 minutes. Slice into 2 inch pieces and serve immediately.

Variation: For a different twist on garlic bread, mix 1 Tbsp of minced garlic and / or granulated garlic for every 3 cups of flour into the wet ingredients and knead.

Pizza Dough

The trick to making excellent pizza dough is to use cold water, not warm water like many recipes call for.

12 Servings	32 Servings	60 Servings	Ingredients
2 Tbsp	5 Tbsp	10 Tbsp	Yeast
5 ¼ cups	14 cups	26 ¼ cups	Cold Water
1 Tbsp	3 Tbsp	5 Tbsp	Sugar
12 cups	32 cups	60 cups	Flour
1 Tbsp	3 Tbsp	5 Tbsp	Salt
12 Tbsp	16 Tbsp	30 Tbsp	Cornmeal
12 Tbsp	16 Tbsp	30 Tbsp	Olive Oil

Directions:

- Combine in a medium bowl yeast, sugar and half of the water. Reserve the remaining amount of water. Quickly mix yeast mixture with a fork for a few seconds.
- Let stand until the yeast starts to bubble to top, about 15-20 minutes. Because you are using cold water the yeast will take longer to dissolve.
- Meanwhile, mix dry ingredients together in a large bowl, sift together and make a well in the center.
- Add wet ingredients to the dry and knead for about 15 minutes. Make sure to really stretch the dough by holding the dough a few inches off the counter and allowing the dough to stretch to the counter top, repeating this a few times.
- In a well-oiled bowl, let dough rise for an hour and a half. Place in a warm area and cover with either plastic wrap or a clean cloth. Meanwhile, prepare ingredients for the pizza.
- Depending on the quantity you are making, use a medium-sized cookie sheet for 12 servings or less and a large cookie sheet for 12 or more servings. Grease cookie sheet and sprinkle with cornmeal.
- Preheat oven to 425°F. Punch down dough and, depending on the size of pizza you are making, divide the dough into quarters or halves.
- Roll dough out onto a floured area and spread evenly by stretching the dough over the cookie sheet. Let rise for another 10 or 15 minutes and spread olive oil over the dough to prevent the dough from becoming soggy when baking.

- Top with pizza sauce, desired toppings and mozzarella. Bake for 20-25 minutes.

Tip: Pre-make pizza dough and have on hand by placing in freezer. Thaw dough 24 hours in fridge before using.

Focaccia

The key to good Focaccia is to have wetter dough than if making regular bread.

12 Servings	32 Servings	60 Servings	Ingredients
1 ½ Tbsp	4 Tbsp	7 Tbsp	Instant Yeast
¾ Tbsp	2 Tbsp	4 Tbsp	Sugar
6 cups	16 cups	30 cups	Warm Water
8 ¼ cups	22 cups	41 ¼ cups	All-purpose Flour
1 Tbsp	3 Tbsp	5 Tbsp	Salt
3 Tbsp	8 Tbsp	15 Tbsp	Olive Oil
1 Tbsp	2 ½ Tbsp	5 Tbsp	Sea Salt

Directions:

- Measure yeast and sugar into the bottom of a medium-sized bowl. Slowly add lukewarm water. Water should be 105 – 110°F.
- Mix yeast, sugar and water together with a fork and wait for yeast to bubble to the surface: approximately 10 minutes.
- Measure dry ingredients into a large bowl and sift together with your hands. Make a well in the center of the dry ingredients and add the yeast mixture. With well-oiled hands, begin mixing ingredients together. It will be stickier than regular dough, as it is a wet dough, so just keep oiling your hands and stretching the dough. Knead for about 15 minutes or until the dough feels stretchable.
- Once you are finished kneading stretch the dough over the sheet pan. Some spots may be thin, but don't worry, it will rise and double in size. Oil the top with olive oil and place plastic wrap over top to prevent the dough from drying out. If you don't add a nice generous coating of oil the plastic will stick to the dough and it will be hard to pull the wrap off the dough.
- Let stand for an hour and a half to two hours or until the dough has doubled in size. To help bread rise, place dough in a warm area where the dough is free from any drafts.
- Push down softly on the top of the dough with your fingers to form indentations.
- Drizzle with olive oil, sea salt and rosemary.
- Pre-heat oven to 425°F and cook Focaccia for approximately 30 minutes or until browned on top.

Other Toppings:

- Sundried Tomatoes & Rosemary
- Black olives &
- Diced Sundried Tomatoes
- Sliced Tomatoes & Rosemary
- Parmesan

Challah Bread

Soft, chewy sweet bread … traditionally served at Christmas dinner. This recipe requires less yeast as it rises quite nicely because of the eggs.

12 Servings	32 Servings	60 Servings	Ingredients
2 Tbsp	5 Tbsp	7 Tbsp	Yeast
1 cup	8 cups	15 cups	Warm Water
1 Tsp	1 Tbsp	3 Tbsp	Sugar
2 Tbsp	1 cup	2 cups	Honey
¼ cup	1 cup	2 cups	Oil
4 (reserve 3 Tbsp)	12 (reserve 9 Tbsp)	30 (reserve 12 Tbsp)	Medium-sized Eggs
1 Tbsp	2 Tbsp	3 Tbsp	Salt
9 cups	22 cups	41 ½ cups	Flour

Directions:

- Measure yeast and sugar into the bottom of a medium-sized bowl. Slowly add lukewarm water. Water should be 105 – 110°F.
- Using a fork, quickly mix yeast, sugar and water together for a few seconds and wait for yeast to bubble to the surface: approximately 10 minutes.
- In another medium-large bowl, beat together eggs, honey and oil and add yeast mixture. Slowly add 2 cups of flour and salt to mixture. Gradually add in remaining flour and knead for 10 minutes. Place dough in a large bowl and cover with plastic wrap. Let rise for an hour and half or until the dough has doubled in size.
- Preheat oven to 375°F. Punch down dough and divide into individual loaves and place in oiled loaf pan. Let rise until the loaves have doubled in size and, just before baking use a pastry brush to spread the remaining egg over the loaves for a golden finish.
- Bake for 35 minutes or until golden brown on top. Check doneness by tapping on the bottom of the loaf; if the loaf sounds hollow than it is done, or check internal temperature with a temperature gauge. Temperature should read 190°F.

Cornbread with Jalapenos & Sweet Corn

Serve as part of a Mexican meal or with your favorite BBQ food items.

12 Servings	32 Servings	60 Servings	Ingredients
2 ¼ cups	6 cups	11 ¼ cups	Cornmeal
3 ¾ cups	10 cups	18 ¾ cups	Milk
3 cups	8 cups	15 cups	Flour
¾ cups	2 cups	3 ¾ cups	Sugar
3 Tbsp	8 Tbsp	15 Tbsp	Baking Powder
1 ½ tsp	4 tsp	7 ½ tsp	Salt
3	8	15	Eggs
¾ cup	2 cup	3 ¾ cup	Vegetable Oil
1 cup	4 cup	7 ½ cup	Sweet Frozen Corn
2 tsp	4 tsp	8 tsp	Fresh or Canned Jalapenos
6 tsp	16 tsp	30 tsp	Paprika

Directions:

- Measure cornmeal and milk into a medium-sized bowl. Let stand for one hour.
- In a large bowl, measure flour, sugar, baking powder and salt and sift together.
- Deseed and mince jalapenos if not already deseeded.
- Add eggs, oil, frozen corn and minced jalapenos to cornmeal and milk mixture. Add wet ingredients to dry mixture and stir.
- Pour mixture into well-oiled loaf pans, muffin tins or individual loaf tins.
- Sprinkle with paprika and bake at 400°F for 30 minutes or until golden brown.

APPETIZERS, DIPS & SPREADS

Hot Crab, Cream Cheese & Sundried Tomato Dip

A subtle crab flavor enhanced with the sweetness of sundried tomatoes. Serve with warmed pita bread.

12 Servings	32 Servings	60 Servings	Ingredients
3 cups	8 cups	15 cups	Cream Cheese
1 cup	3 cups	5 cups	Heavy Cream
1 Tbsp	3 Tbsp	5 Tbsp	Worcestershire Sauce
2 - 184 g cans	5 - 184 g cans	7 - 184 g cans	Flaked Canned Crab
1 cup	3 cups	5 cups	Sundried Tomatoes in oil
1 Tbsp	3 Tbsp	5 Tbsp	Juice from Lemon
½ tsp	½ Tbsp	1 ½ Tbsp	Sea Salt (or to taste)
½ tsp	½ Tbsp	1 ½ Tbsp	Pepper (or to taste)

Directions:

- Chop sundried tomatoes into small pieces.
- In a large bowl, mix together cream cheese, crab, sundried tomatoes, salt, pepper and lemon juice. I find it easiest to mix with your hands.
- Place in a medium-sized sauce pan, add cream and heat over medium low until the cream cheese has melted and the cream has blended in and the dip is bubbling. Stir constantly to prevent burning.
- Serve hot with crackers, pita bread or naan bread.

Hot Artichoke & Asiago Dip

A delicious blend of cheeses and flavor packed artichokes sure to please anyone.

12 Servings	32 Servings	60 Servings	Ingredients
2 - 540 ml	4 - 540 ml	8 - 540 ml	Canned Artichokes
8 oz	12 oz	16 oz	Shredded Asiago cheese
2 cups	4 cups	6 cups	Shredded Parmesan cheese
2 - 8 oz	3 - 8 oz	4 - 8 oz	Packages of cream cheese
1whole	3 whole	5 whole	Lemons
1 Tbsp	3 Tbsp	5 Tbsp	Worcestershire sauce
1 tsp	2 tsp	3 tsp	Cayenne spice, or to taste
1 tsp	1 Tbsp	2 Tbsp	Sea Salt, or to taste
1 tsp	1 Tbsp	2 Tbsp	Pepper to taste

Directions:

- In a food processor, blend artichokes, then in a medium-sized bowl combine with cheeses. Using a spatula, spoon mixture into a medium sauce pan and melt together over low heat.
- Once cheese is melted, add lemon juice, salt, pepper, cayenne spice and Worcestershire to taste.
- Serve hot with crackers or pita bread.
- Keep refrigerated and heat when needed.

Guacamole

A fresh Mexican dip with the zesty flavour of lime and cilantro, sure to be gobbled up time after time.

12 Servings	32 Servings	60 Servings	Ingredients
6 ripe	16	30	Avocados
1 sprig	3 sprigs	6 sprigs	Green Onion
2 cloves	4 cloves	7 cloves	Minced Garlic
1 Tbsp	2 Tbsp	4 Tbsp	Taco Seasoning
6 Tbsp	10 Tbsp	15 Tbsp	Lime Juice (fresh or from concentrate)
½ Tbsp	1 ½ Tbsp	2 Tbsp	Sea Salt, or to taste
1 pinch	2 pinch	3 pinch	Cayenne spice, or to taste
1whole	3 whole	5 whole	Fresh Diced Tomato
2 Tbsp	4 Tbsp	6 Tbsp	Cilantro

Directions:

- In a food processor, combine avocados, green onion, garlic, taco seasoning, lime juice and salt. Using a spatula scrape the guacamole out of the bowl and place into a separate plastic or glass bowl.
- Add cayenne, diced tomatoes and cilantro and stir.
- Season to taste.
- Serve with tortilla chips, quesadillas or burritos.

Tzatziki

This tangy dip with a hint of dill will add a blast of flavour to any Greek dish. Serve with pita chips, Souvlaki or Moussaka.

12 Servings	32 Servings	60 Servings	Ingredients
1 ½ cups	4 cups	7 ½ cups	Plain Greek Yogurt
1/2 cup	1 1/4 cup	2 1/2 cups	Sour cream
1 ½ cups	4 cups	7 ½ cups	Grated Cucumber
2-3 Tbsp	3-4 Tbsp	4-5 Tbsp	Lemon Juice (Fresh or Concentrate)
3-4 cloves	5-6 cloves	6-7 cloves	Crushed Garlic
1 Tbsp	2 Tbsp	4 Tbsp	Dill
1 Tbsp	2 Tbsp	3 Tbsp	Sea Salt, or to taste
1 Tbsp	2 Tbsp	3 Tbsp	Pepper, or to taste

Directions:

- In a food processor, blend together peeled garlic, minced dill, Greek style yogurt, lemon juice, salt and pepper.
- Adjust flavors to suit, using a spatula scrape tzatziki into either a glass or plastic bowl (non-metallic) and add grated cucumber (Drain the excess water from the grated cucumber if there is any). Refrigerate for at least a couple of hours to let the flavors merge.
- Use Greek style yogurt as it is not as runny as regular yogurt, however if you cannot find Greek style yogurt at your local super market, then use regular yogurt and drain off any excess liquid.

Mexican Cream Cheese & Salsa Rolls

These yummy rolls are extremely easy to make and really satisfying to any taste bud.

12 Servings	32 Servings	60 Servings	Ingredients
5	15	28	Whole wheat or Plain tortilla wraps
1 250 g	1 ½ - 250 g	3 – 250 g	Packages of cream cheese
3	5	10	Large ripe tomatoes
1 head	1 ½ heads	2 heads	Romaine Lettuce
1 – 398 ml can	2 – 398 ml cans	3 – 398 ml cans	Black Sliced Olives
1 cup	3 cups	5 cups	Salsa

Directions:

- Dice tomatoes into small pieces, cut lettuce down the middle and slice into thin horizontal strips. Set aside.
- Drain and rinse olives and set aside.
- Spread cream cheese over tortilla, spread salsa over cream cheese, add tomatoes, olives and lettuce to the middle of the tortilla.
- Fold the end of the tortilla closest to you over the ingredients and pull towards you, then roll the tortilla and cut into ¼ inch pieces.

7 Layer Dip

Requested often and very seldom to have left-overs with this yummy Mexican favorite.

12 Servings	32 Servings	60 Servings	Ingredients
1 ½ cups	4 cups	7 cups	Sour Cream
1 ½ cups	4 cups	7 cups	Guacamole
1 ½ cups	4 cups	7 cups	Refried Beans
1 ½ cups	4 cups	7 cups	Medium Salsa
1 cup	3 cups	5 cups	Monterey Jack Cheese
1 cup	3 cups	5 cups	Green Onions
1 cup	3 cups	5 cups	Canned Sliced Black Olives

Directions:

- Follow recipe instructions for Guacamole.
- Wash and dice green onions. Drain sliced black olives.
- Grate cheese and set aside.
- Heat refried beans and purée into a smooth consistency. Let cool.
- Using a large rectangular pan, layer dip as follows: refried beans on the bottom, then guacamole, followed by sour cream, salsa, cheese and top off with green onion and olives. Refrigerate for an hour before serving. Serve with tortilla chips.

Thai Salad Rolls

Might take a couple tries to get the rolling right, but with a little patience and a few tries you will be a rolling pro. Want to know the difference between glass vermicelli and cellophane mung bean noodles? Glass vermicelli is made of rice and cellophane noodles are made from the starch of mung beans and are called cellophane because of their resemblance to cellophane.

12 Servings	32 Servings	60 Servings	Ingredients
12	32	60	Rice paper wraps
200 g	454 g	900 g	Glass Vermicelli or Cellophane Mung Bean Noodles
3	8	15	Carrots
3	8	15	Cucumbers
1 ½ heads	3 heads	6 heads	Red Leaf Lettuce
1½ cups	3 cups	8 cups	Fresh Basil
1½ cups	3 cups	8 cups	Fresh Cilantro
1½ cups	3 cups	8 cups	Fresh Mint
6 sprigs	12 sprigs	24 sprigs	Scallion
6 Tbsp	¾ cup	1 ¼ cups	Thai Sweet Hot Sauce
1 cup	2 cup	5 cups	Pea Shoots or Sprouts
2 tsp	1 Tbsp	2 Tbsp	Salt (or to taste)
3 Tbsp	8 Tbsp	¾ Cup	Lime Juice (Fresh or from concentrate)
12 cups	12 cups	12 cups	Hot Water

Directions:

- Heat water in tea kettle. Once boiling, pour over glass vermicelli noodles and soak until soft (about 10 minutes). Another method is to boil water in a pot and, once water reaches boiling temperature, turn stove off, add noodles and put lid on pot and steam until soft, then drain and rinse with cold water.
- Julienne carrots and cucumbers into ¼ of an inch matchsticks and set aside. Or you can use a peeler and peel the carrot and cucumber until it is down to its core.
- Wash and mince the mint, basil and cilantro. Wash scallions and dice diagonally into small pieces.

- In a medium-sized bowl, mix together the carrots, cucumber, pea shoots, cooled vermicelli noodles, scallions, minced cilantro, basil and mint, lime juice and salt.
- Cut the lettuce in half and then half again. You want lettuce pieces big enough to wrap the ingredients into. Wash and set aside.
- Boil water in tea kettle again and pour into large bowl. Let cool enough so you can stick your hand into the water without scalding yourself.
- Soak the rice paper for about 20 seconds or until soft. It should become transparent. Once soft, lay the ricepaper on a clean towel or a piece of paper towel which will help soak up some of the excess water.
- Add ingredients beginning with lettuce, layer with basil, and then add the vermicelli noodle mixture.
- Beginning with the top portion of the rice paper, roll over the ingredients towards the middle of the paper and tuck under by pulling the roll towards you.
- Grab the sides and flip inwards towards the middle, overlapping the first section that was rolled. Finish rolling by pushing the roll away from you until the bottom portion of the roll is stuck to the rest of the roll. Wet your knife and cut on a diagonal.
- Serve with peanut sauce, hoisin sauce (cut with hot water) or Thai Sweet & Hot Sauce.

Sundried Tomato & Fennel Spanakopita

A unique twist on a traditional Greek dish. You can make the spanakopita to your desired size whether you want to serve them as an appetizer or a main dish.

12 Servings	32 Servings	60 Servings	Ingredients
1-454 g package	4 -454 g packages	8 -454 g packages	Phyllo Pastry
2 -300 g packages	4 - 300 g packages	7 - 300 g packages	Frozen Spinach
3 cups	9 cups	13 cups	Feta
1 Tbsp	3 Tbsp	5 Tbsp	Crushed Fennel
1 ½ cup	2 cups	3 cups	Sundried Tomatoes
1 Tbsp	3 Tbsp	5 Tbsp	Lemon Juice
¼ cup	1 cup	2 cups	Melted Butter
1 tsp	1 Tbsp	2 Tbsp	Pepper

Directions:

- Thaw phyllo pastry according to package instructions. As well, thaw frozen spinach and be sure to drain it really well.
- In a food processor, pulse sundried tomatoes.
- Mix spinach, feta, crushed fennel, sundried tomatoes, lemon juice and pepper together.
- Melt butter on low and set aside.
- Roll out phyllo pastry and place two onto top of each other. Cover rest of phyllo up with damp cloth.
- Place a couple of tablespoons of feta and spinach mixture together in the middle of the phyllo sheets and fold the longer side of phyllo over and brush with butter.
- Fold both outer sides over and fold the whole thing over again.
- Brush with butter and bake for 30 minutes or until golden brown.
- Serve with tzatziki.

Samosas

Instead of making your own dough which is traditionally used, this recipe calls for puff pastry which makes for a savory samosas that is bake instead of fried.

12 Servings	32 Servings	60 Servings	Ingredients
8	25	50	Potatoes
2 Tbsp	5 Tbsp	7 Tbsp	Finely chopped fresh Gingerroot
1 Tbsp	3 Tbsp	5 Tbsp	Crushed fresh Garlic
2 tsp	2 Tbsp	4 Tbsp	Cumin Seeds
1 ½ tsp	1 Tbsp	2 Tbsp	Mustard Seeds
2 Tbsp	4 Tbsp	5 Tbsp	Garam Masala
1 Tbsp	3 Tbsp	4 Tbsp	Mild Curry
½ Tbsp	2 Tbsp	4 Tbsp	Sea Salt (or to taste)
1 tsp	2 tsp	3 tsp	Minced Fresh Green or Red Chilies
2 Tbsp	4 Tbsp	6 Tbsp	Fresh Corianders (chopped)
2 Tbsp	4 Tbsp	6 Tbsp	Lemon Juice
1 ½ cups	3 cups	5 cups	Thawed Green Peas
2 - 450 g	6 - 250 g	10 - 250 g	Puff Pastry Packages
2	6	10	Eggs

Directions:

- Thaw puff pastry 1 hour before using.
- To make filling, cook diced potatoes in boiling salted water until tender. Drain and mash together.
- In a large frying pan, heat ghee and sauté minced garlic, ginger, cumin and mustard seeds, salt, garam masala, curry, frozen peas and diced chillies. Add potatoes, lemon juice and coriander.
- Mix above ingredients together.
- Roll out thawed puff pastry and cut into 9 pieces. Add a tablespoon of mixture into the center of the pastry and fold top corner over to bottom of corner and pinch sides of the seam together.

- Preheat oven to 400°F. Lightly coat samosas with beaten egg. Line baking sheet with parchment paper and bake in oven for 30 minutes or until golden brown.

Variation – Substitute puff pastry with wonton wrappers and deep fry in oil until crispy and brown on the outside.

Pakoras

You can find chick pea flour or garbanzo flour at most supermarkets in the Ethnic aisle. Bet you can't eat just one!

12 Servings	32 Servings	60 Servings	Ingredients
9 cups	12 cups	22 cups	Chick Pea Flour
2 cups	6 cups	12 cups	Water (approximately)
2 Tbsp	4 Tbsp	8 Tbsp	Garam Masala
1 Tbsp	2 Tbsp	4 Tbsp	Garlic Powder
3-4 tsp	6-8 tsp	8-10 tsp	Chili Powder or Cayenne Pepper (or to taste)
1 Tbsp	3 Tbsp	5 Tbsp	Cumin Seeds
1 Tbsp	2 ½ Tbsp	4 Tbsp	Baking Powder
1 Tbsp	2 ½ Tbsp	4 Tbsp	Salt
4 cups	10 cups	17 cups	Fresh Spinach, Onions, Cauliflower or Potato
9 cups	12 cups	15 cups	Oil (approximately, for deep frying)

Directions:

- Mix together chick pea flour, garam masala, garlic powder, chilli powder, cumin seeds, baking powder and salt. Gradually add water and beat mixture with a wooden spoon until fluffy.
- Add vegetables to batter and mix thoroughly. Vegetables should be thinly coated. Heat oil until 375°F (about 15 minutes).
- Drop batter, tablespoon by tablespoon, into hot oil, careful to not overcrowd. Fry on both sides until golden brown (approx 2-3 minutes).
- Remove with a slotted spoon and drain thoroughly on paper towels.
- Serve with chutney of your choice.

Chopped Black Olive Spread

This rich tapenade is simply delicious as a dip for crackers or even as a sandwich spread.

12 Servings	32 Servings	60 Servings	Ingredients
2 cups	5 cups	7 ½	Oil Cured Black Olives
2 cups	5 cups	7 ½	Pitted Black Olives
7 ½ Tbsp	1 ¼ cup	2 cups	Olive Oil
2 cloves	4 cloves	7 cloves	Garlic
½ tsp each	2 tsp each	1 Tbsp each	Dried Oregano, Basil, Thyme, and Rosemary

Directions:

- Pit the oil-cured olives one at a time by placing each on a cutting board and resting the flat side of a large knife on it. Thump the knife with the heel of your hand. The pit can then be easily removed.
- Drain the canned olives in a strainer and shake out all the liquid.
- Combine olives, garlic, herbs and olive oil in a blender and process until a spreadable texture has formed.
- Serve with crackers, or makes a great addition to any lunch table.

Variation – Spread leftover olive spread on thawed puff pastry and roll into a log and bake at 400 F until golden brown. Let cool and slice into thin pinwheels.

Hot Broccoli Dip

This dip is sooo yummy and is sure to be gobbled up!

12 Servings	32 Servings	60 Servings	Ingredients
1 cup	5 cups	7 cups	Finely Diced Broccoli Crowns
1 cup	5 cups	7 cups	Finely Diced Onions
1 cup	5 cups	7 cups	Finely Diced Mush-rooms
3 Tbsp	7 Tbsp	¼ cup	Grapeseed Oil or non-hydrogenated Canola Oil
½ cup	1 ½ cup	2 cups	Sour Cream
2 248 ml	3 248 ml	4 248 ml	Canned Cream of Mushroom Soup
3 cups	5 cups	7 ½ cups	Grated Sharp Cheddar Cheese
1 ½ tsp	3 Tbsp	5 Tbsp	Worcestershire Sauce
¾ tsp	1 ½ tsp	1 Tbsp	Hot Paprika Powder (or to taste)
1 tsp	1 Tbsp	3 Tbsp	Garlic Powder
1 tsp	1 Tbsp	1 ½ Tbsp	Sea Salt (or to taste)
1 tsp	1 Tbsp	1 ½ Tbsp	Pepper (or to taste)

Directions:

- Wash broccoli and mushrooms well and set aside. Peel onion and slice in half.
- Finely dice broccoli, onions and mushrooms. In a large frying pan over medium heat, sauté veggies in oil until soft. Add the cream of mushroom soup, grated cheese, sour cream, Worcestershire sauce, garlic powder, hot paprika, sea salt and pepper. Heat until bubbling and the cheese has melted.
- Serve in a bread bowl.

Bean & Salsa Dip

Use this savory dip in your favorite Mexican taco, fajita or with tortillas chips.

12 Servings	32 Servings	60 Servings	Ingredients
3 cups	8 cups	15 cups	Kidney Beans
3 Tbsp	8 Tbsp	15 Tbsp	Olive Oil
3 -4 Tbsp	5 -6 Tbsp	6 -7 Tbsp	Water
1 cup	2 cups	3 cups	Medium Salsa
1 Tbsp	3 Tbsp	5 Tbsp	Chili Powder
1 Tbsp	3 Tbsp	5 Tbsp	Ground Cumin
1 Tbsp	3 Tbsp	5 Tbsp	Fresh Parsley or Cilantro

Directions:

- Combine beans, oil and water in a food processor and blend until almost smooth. Add cumin and chili powder, season to taste and add extra water if needed. Blend into a smooth consistency.
- Scrape mixture into a bowl.
- Add salsa and fresh herbs to mixture.
- Serve with hot pita triangles or taco chips.

Variation: Add shredded monterey jack or cheddar cheese to bean mixture and heat in a medium-sized pan until cheese is melted. Scrape into a serving dish add salsa and fresh herbs. Serve immediately with taco chips.

Spinach Dip

One of my favorites… Not a low fat dip but when it tastes this good – who cares!

12 Servings	32 Servings	60 Servings	Ingredients
2 300 g	4 300 g	6 300 g	Packaged Frozen Chopped Spinach
2 cup	4 cups	6 cups	Sour Cream
1 cup	2 cups	4 cups	Mayonnaise
1 - 40 g	1 ½ 40 g	2 - 40 g	Packaged Dehydrated Vegetable Soup or Onion Soup mix
1 Tbsp	3 Tbsp	5 Tbsp	Worcestershire Sauce
¼ cup	¾ cup	1 cup	Finely diced Red Onion or Chives
2 - 6 oz cans	3 - 6 oz cans	4 - 6 oz cans	Sliced Water Chestnuts or Artichoke Hearts
2 loaves	5 loaves	8 loaves	Round French Bread

Directions:

- Thaw frozen spinach and drain really well.
- Combine all ingredients in a food processor, except the bread and blend. Adjust the seasonings to taste.
- Hollow out the round loaf and fill with dip.
- Cube the bread you removed and remaining bread and use to dip.
- Can also serve with veggies.

Chick Pea Pâté

A protein packed pate that can be served with crackers or as an addition to sandwiches. Try experimenting with your favourite ingredients to come up with your own pate at your next dinner party!

12 Servings	32 Servings	60 Servings	Ingredients
2 398 ml	3 398 ml	4 398 ml	Canned Chick Peas (drained, rinsed and mashed)
½ cup	1 cup	1 ½ cups	Water
1 cup	1 ½ cups	2 cups	Nutritional Yeast
2 tsp	2 Tbsp	4 Tbsp	Minced Garlic
4Tbsp	6 Tbsp	8 Tbsp	Lemon Juice
4 sprigs	5 sprigs	6 sprigs	Green Onion
2 stalks	3 stalks	4 stalks	Celery Sticks
2	3	4	Carrots
1	2	3	Red Peppers
2 tsp	3 Tbsp	5 Tbsp	Braggs Seasoning
¾ tsp	2 Tbsp	3 Tbsp	Thyme
¾ tsp	2 Tbsp	3 Tbsp	Basil
¾ tsp	2 Tbsp	3 Tbsp	Sage
½ tsp	1/2 Tbsp	1 Tbsp	Salt (or to taste)
½ tsp	1 Tbsp	2 Tbsp	Pepper (or to taste)

Directions:

- Drain, rinse and purée chick peas with water, lemon juice and Braggs seasoning in a food processor.
- Finely dice red pepper and green onion. Grate celery and carrot. Mince garlic and set aside.
- Mix all ingredients together.
- Preheat oven to 350˚F and divide pâté batter into a few 9 x 9 inch baking dishes or bread pans. By dividing the pâté into a couple of baking dishes or bread pans, you can freeze any left-over pâté and it won't take up a lot of room in the freezer.
- Bake pâté for approximately 45 minutes or until top is golden brown.
- Let cool and serve with crackers or as a sandwich spread.

Spinach & Basil Pesto

Makes a lovely sandwich spread, pasta sauce or even add to eggs. Substitute spinach for basil if basil is unavailable and use walnuts, which are a cheaper alternative to pine nuts.

12 Servings	32 Servings	60 Servings	Ingredients
6 cups	16 cups	30 cups	Basil and / or Spinach
6 cloves	9 cloves	12 cloves	Crushed Garlic
3 cups	8 cups	15 cups	Walnuts
3 cups	8 cups	15 cups	Olive Oil
3 cups	8 cups	15 cups	Parmesan Cheese
3/4 cups	2 cups	3 ½ cups	Romano Cheese
3 Tbsp	8 Tbsp	15 Tbsp	Fresh Lemon Juice
¾ tsp	2 tsp	1 Tbsp	Sea Salt (or to taste)
¾ tsp	2 tsp	1 Tbsp	Pepper (or to taste)

Directions:

- Combine all ingredients in food processor and blend together.
- Substitute spinach for basil if it is hard to find enough basil to make enough for large quantities. Season to taste.
- Serve as a sandwhich spread or over hot pasta noodles and top with fresh grated romano and parmesan.

Artichoke Pâté

A simply satisfying pâté that will leave you wanting more.

12 Servings	32 Servings	60 Servings	Ingredients
4 ½ cups	12 cups	22 ½ cups	Canned Artichoke Hearts
¾ cups	2 cups	4 cups	Mayonnaise
1 ½ cups	4 cups	7 ½ cups	Parmesan
1 ½ cups	4 cups	7 ½ cups	Cream cheese
3 Tbsp	8 Tbsp	15 Tbsp	Lemon juice
3	5	7	Garlic cloves
¾ tsp	½ Tbsp	1 Tbsp	Cayenne Pepper (or to taste)

Directions:

- Preheat oven to 400°F.
- Combine artichoke hearts, mayo, parmesan and cream cheese together in a food processor.
- Add the remaining ingredients and blend. Using a spatula scrape into an oven proof baking dish.
- Bake at 400°F for 30 minutes.
- Serve with crackers.

Hummus

A classic Middle Eastern dish, full of protein and low in fat. Serve with crackers, veggies or as a sandwich spread.

12 Servings	32 Servings	60 Servings	Ingredients
2 - 398 ml cans	3 - 398 ml cans	1 - 2.4 L can	Chick Peas
2-3 cloves	3-4 cloves	4-5 cloves	Garlic
2 sprigs	3 sprigs	4 sprigs	Green Onion
2 Tbsp	5 Tbsp	8 Tbsp	Cumin
1 whole	2 whole	4 whole	Lemons
½ Tbsp	1 Tbsp	2 Tbsp	Sea Salt, or to taste
½ cup	¾ cup	1 cup	Olive Oil
½ cup	1 cup	1 ½ cups	Tahini or Peanut Butter
1 Tbsp	5 Tbsp	8 Tbsp	Parsley
1 Tbsp	3 Tbsp	5 Tbsp	Maple Syrup (optional)

Directions:

- Rinse chick peas under cold water.
- Combine all of the ingredients in a food processor and blend until smooth; add more liquid if too thick (olive oil and/or water) until desired consistency is reached.
- For a different flavor try adding roasted red pepper or hot sauce.

Baba Gannuj

The best baba gannuj I ever had was in Egypt, so delicious, so I wanted to create the same taste. Try adding a few drops of liquid smoke for a subtle smokey flavor.

12 Servings	32 Servings	60 Servings	Ingredients
2	4	6	Eggplant
¾ cup	2 cups	4 cups	Tahini
1 tsp	2 tsp	3 tsp	Liquid Smoke
4 cloves	6 cloves	8 cloves	Roasted Garlic
3-4 Tbsp	4-5 Tbsp	5-6 Tbsp	Water
2 small	3 small	4 small	Roma Tomato
3 tsp	6 tsp	8 tsp	Fresh Chopped Cilantro
3 Tbsp	8 Tbsp	15 Tbsp	Olive Oil
1 Tbsp	3 Tbsp	5 Tbsp	Lemon Juice
¾ tsp	1 tsp	1 ½ tsp	Salt

Directions:

- Slice the eggplant in half lengthwise and sprinkle salt on it. Let sit for 20 minutes until the salt draws out the bitterness; then pat dry with paper towel.
- Bake eggplant and whole garlic at 400°F until eggplant is soft enough to pull the skin off, the garlic bulb is golden brown and the cloves are soft enough to squeeze out of the bulb.
- Add the following ingredients to a blender: eggplant, garlic, liquid smoke, lemon juice, salt and olive oil. Process in blender until smooth. Scrape into a bowl.
- Dice tomatoes and finely chop cilantro and add to mixture. Serve chilled with warm pita bread.

Vegan Black Bean Spread

You will hardly notice the tofu and is a nice low fat alternative to calorie laden dips.

12 Servings	32 Servings	60 Servings	Ingredients
2 - 398 ml cans	3 - 398 ml cans	4 - 398 ml cans	Black Beans (drained)
1 - 350 g	1 ½ - 350 g	2 - 350 g	Medium-firm Tofu
2-3 cloves	3-4 cloves	4-5 cloves	Garlic
1 Tbsp	3 Tbsp	5 Tbsp	Cumin
2 sprigs	3 sprigs	4 sprigs	Green Onions
½ tsp	1 tsp	1 ½ tsp	Salt
2 Tbsp	3 Tbsp	4 Tbsp	Olive Oil
2 tsp	1 Tbsp	2 Tbsp	Lemon Juice
1 tsp	2 tsp	4 tsp	Maple Syrup (optional)

Directions:

- Combine all ingredients in a food processor and mix until the flavors merge. Adjust seasonings to your taste.
- Use quickly as this dish will only keep for a couple of days in the fridge.
- You can omit the tofu and process with just black beans.
- Add fresh dill for a different flavor.

Vegan Pâté

A simply irresistible pâté with a nice earthy flavour.

12 Servings	32 Servings	60 Servings	Ingredients
4 ½ cups	12 cups	22 ½ cups	Ground Sunflower Seeds or Walnuts
1/2 cup	2 cups	3 cups	Bread crumbs
1 cup	3 cups	5 cups	Nutritional Yeast
3	8	15	Large Carrots
3	8	15	Large Potato
3	8	15	Large Celery stalks
12	32	60	Large Brown Mush-rooms
3 Tbsp	6 Tbsp	9 Tbsp	Lemon Juice
1 Tbsp	3 Tbsp	5 Tbsp	Tamari
6 Tbsp	8 Tbsp	10 Tbsp	Olive Oil
1 ½	2	2 ½	Onion
1 tsp	2 tsp	4 tsp	Salt
1 tsp	2 tsp	4 tsp	Pepper
1 Tbsp	3 Tbsp	5 Tbsp	Basil
1 Tbsp	3 Tbsp	5 Tbsp	Thyme
1 Tbsp	3 Tbsp	5 Tbsp	Sage

Directions:

- Grate carrots, potatoes, and celery. Dice onions and mushrooms.
- In a large frying pan over medium heat, sautee vegetables in oil until soft. In a food processor, combine vegetables, sunflower seeds or walnuts, nutritional yesat and bread crumbs Add salt, pepper, sage, basil, thyme, tamari and lemon juice.
- Mix all ingredients together and divide into a couple of greased 9 x 9 inch baking dish or bread pans and bake at 350°F until edges turn brown and shrink from the sides of the pan.
- Serve with crackers or in a wrap.

Tuna Salad

A great addition to any lunch table. Try adding different vegetables such as diced red pepper.

12 Servings	32 Servings	60 Servings	Ingredients
1 - 184 g can	1 - 1.4 L can	2 - 1.4 L can	Tuna
6 Tbsp	1 cup	1 ½ cups	Real Mayonnaise or Miracle Whip
1	4	8	Celery Stalk (finely chopped)
4 stalks	8 stalks	12 stalks	Green Onion
½ tsp	½ Tbsp	1 Tbsp	Sea Salt, or to taste
2 tsp	5 tsp	8 tsp	Pepper, or to taste
1	3	4	Grated Dill Pickle
1 Tbsp	3 Tbsp	5 Tbsp	Chopped Fresh Dill

Directions:

- Drain tuna into a strainer to remove any excess juices.
- Finely dice celery and green onion. Grate dill pickle into a bowl. If using fresh dill, finely dice and place in bowl. Add celery and green onion.
- Add tuna to the bowl, flake apart tuna and mix with other ingredients. Add salt and pepper, taste and adjust accordingly. Add more mayo if the mixture is too dry.
- You may wonder what the difference is between Miracle Whip and real mayo. Miracle whip has a lot more sugar, and therefore is sweeter in flavor, while real mayo has almost no sweet taste to it. I prefer using real mayo in egg and tuna salads to cut down on that overly sweet taste.

Egg Salad

A yummy protein alternative for vegetarians and is a great way to use up any left-over hard boiled eggs.

12 Servings	32 Servings	60 Servings	Ingredients
12	32	60	Hard Boiled Eggs
6 Tbsp	1 ½ cups	3 cups	Miracle Whip or Mayonnaise
1	1 ½	2	Red Onion or Green Onion (finely diced)
1	1 ½	2	Red Pepper/Avocado (optional)
1 ½ tsp	1 Tbsp	1 ½ Tbsp	Salt (or to taste)
1 ½ tsp	1 Tbsp	1 ½ Tbsp	Pepper (or to taste)

Directions:

- Place eggs in a large pot with cold water. Add either 1/2 a teaspoon of salt or vinegar for every cup of water added. This will allow for easier peeling.
- Over medium heat, softly boil eggs over for 10-12 minutes. Turn off element and let sit for another 6-8 minutes.
- Rinse the eggs under cold water and then peel.
- With a pastry blender, mash eggs together. Add mayo, salt and pepper and mix together.
- Finely chop onion and add to egg salad mixture. Adjust seasoning and mayo accordingly.
- Add finely diced red pepper or try avocado for a different twist.

Garlic Butter

Use this spread on fresh French bread and toast in the oven and serve warm with Spaghetti or Lasagna. I often find myself doubling up even more on this one as this recipe comes in handy when sautéing veggies like green beans on the grill.

12 Servings	32 Servings	60 Servings	Ingredients
3 cups	7 cups	12 cups	Butter or non- hydrogenated Margarine
2 Tbsp	5 Tbsp	7 Tbsp	Minced Garlic
1 Tbsp	2 Tbsp	4 Tbsp	Granulated Garlic Powder
3 Tbsp	5 Tbsp	8 Tbsp	Fresh Parsley

Directions:

- Finely mince garlic and fresh parsley.
- Using an electric mixer whip butter or margarine with minced garlic, granulated garlic powder and parsley until smooth.
- Use as a spread for garlic toast or for sautéing veggies.
- Will keep in the fridge for up to 10 days.

Chipotle Mayo

Remember to glove up when deseeding these hot peppers and wash the cutting board really well after to help rid of any left-over spiciness from the peppers.

12 Servings	32 Servings	60 Servings	Ingredients
4-5	7-8	10-11	Chipotle Pepper
1 ½ cups	4 cups	7 cups	Mayonnaise

Directions:

- Using gloves cut the chipotle peppers in half and deseed the chipotle peppers by running the back of your knife along the membrane to pull the seeds away from the pepper. Mince peppers very finely.
- Using a hand blender, blend until pepper is completely mixed in with mayo.
- Serve with sweet potato fries or as a sandwich spread.

Pesto Mayo

Makes an excellent sandwich spread.

12 Servings	32 Servings	60 Servings	Ingredients
9 Tbsp	1 ¼ cup	2 cups	Pesto
1 ½ cups	4 cups	7 cups	Mayonnaise

Directions:

- Using a hand held blender mix either pre-bought or home-made pesto with mayonnaise until well blended.
- Use as a sandwich spread.
- Will keep for up to a week in the fridge.

Sundried Tomato Mayo

Use sundried tomatoes packed in oil rather than dried ones, saves time having to rehydrate them and they have more flavour.

12 Servings	32 Servings	60 Servings	Ingredients
¼ cup	1 cup	1 ½ cups	Sundried Tomatoes
1 ½ cups	4 cups	7 cups	Mayonnaise

Directions:

- Using a hand held blender purée sundried tomatoes with mayonnaise until well blended. Add more or less mayo according to your tastes.
- Use as a sandwich spread or on crackers.

Gomashi Tofu Slices

These tofu slices work great as a sandwich filler or are super yummy on their own! Makes a nice breakfast alternative for vegetarians and vegans.

12 Servings	32 Servings	60 Servings	Ingredients
1350 g	3350 g	5350 g	Medium Firm Tofu
1 Tbsp	3 Tbsp	6 Tbsp	Sesame Oil
2 Tbsp	7 Tbsp	12 Tbsp	Braggs Sauce
1 Tbsp	5 Tbsp	8 Tbsp	Tamari
3 Tbsp	½ cup	¾ cup	Gomashi*

Gomashi is a Japanese mixture of roasted sesame seeds; available at health food stores.

Directions:

- Slice tofu lengthwise into a ¼ inch pieces.
- In a medium sauce pan, heat sesame oil.
- Add tofu to pan. Cook the tofu in batches as both sides need to be browned.
- Add Braggs, tamari and Gomashi.
- Fry on both sides until lightly browned.
- Can be stored in fridge for a couple of days.

SAUCES, GRAVIES & BREAD CRUMBS

Mushroom Miso Gravy

Use this delicious gravy on mashed potatoes or on Shepherd's pie.

12 Servings	32 Servings	60 Servings	Ingredients
2 Tbsp	4 Tbsp	6 Tbsp	Olive Oil
1 small	2 small	3 small	Onions
1-2 cloves	3-4 cloves	5-6 cloves	Minced Garlic
6 -7	8 -9	10 -11	Brown Mushrooms
6 Tbsp	½ cup	1 cup	Tamari
½ cup	1 cup	2 cups	Miso (either white, red or brown)
1 ½ cups	4 cups	7 cups	Water
¼ cup	¾ cup	1 cup	Rice Vinegar or Balsamic
2 Tbsp	4 Tbsp	6 Tbsp	Arrowroot or Spelt Flour

Directions:

- In a medium-sized pan heat oil. Finely mince onions and garlic. Wash mushrooms well and slice thinly. Sautee onions, garlic and mushrooms until caramelized.
- Meanwhile, using a food processor, blend together tamari, miso paste, water and vinegar.
- Add blended mixture to the sautéed onions and garlic.
- Simmer on low heat for 35 minutes, stirring frequently.
- If it needs to be thickened, sift arrowroot flour or spelt flour into the gravy and whisk briskly to avoid clumping.

A note about miso pastes: Depending on the type of miso you use, it will give your gravy a different flavor. White miso will be lighter in flavor and therefore you may want to adjust the quantity of miso used. A darker miso such as brown or red will give your gravy a more robust flavor.

Glico Japanese Gravy with Miso

Glico Japanese Curry has a mild curry flavor and is delicious as a gravy, or simply add root vegetables to the curry to make a wonderful curried stew. Glico Curry is available at Asian supermarkets or large supermarket chains.

12 Servings	32 Servings	60 Servings	Ingredients
3 Tbsp	8 Tbsp	15 Tbsp	Miso
½ package	1 packages	2 packages	Glico Curry Cubes
2-3 cups	5-6 cups	8-9 cups	Hot Water
1 tsp	2 tsp	3 tsp	Pepper or To Taste
2 tsp	4 tsp	8 tsp	Fennel (crushed)
1 Tbsp	3 Tbsp	5 Tbsp	Rice Wine Vinegar, Red Wine Vinegar or Balsamic

Directions:

- In a medium-sized sauce pan, heat water to a simmer. Add Glico curry cubes.
- Melt Glico curry cubes in a hot water. Once melted turn down to a low temperature and add miso paste (do not boil miso as it will separate).
- Whisk the miso paste in with the Glico. If you having a hard time incorporating the two you may find a hand held blender works or a food processor.
- Add vinegar, salt and pepper.
- Using a mortar and pestle, crush fennel and add to above ingredients.
- Serve over potatoes, Shepherd's Pie or stew.

Mango, Cilantro & Red Onion Salsa

This sweet dish makes an excellent accompaniment for spicy Thai Green Curry.

12 Servings	32 Servings	60 Servings	Ingredients
3	8	15	Mango Semi Ripe
6 Tbsp	¾ cup	1 ¼ cups	Fresh Cilantro or to taste
2	3	4	Red Onion
1 Tbsp	2 Tbsp	3 Tbsp	Thai Sweet Chili Sauce

Directions:

- Using a small paring knife, peel mango and dice into small pieces.
- Peel and dice red onion into small pieces.
- Wash and finely mince cilantro. Cilantro is either hated or loved; you can make this dish according to your taste and add more or less.
- Toss the above with Thai Sweet Chili Sauce (available at most supermarkets) and serve with green curry.

Balsamic Croutons

Adds a little excitement to traditional Caesar Salad.

12 Servings	32 Servings	60 Servings	Ingredients
6	16	30	Left- Over Bread Slices
¾ cup	1 cups	1 ¼ cups	Olive Oil
6 Tbsp	½ cup	¾ cup	Balsamic Vinegar
3 Tbsp	5 Tbsp	8 Tbsp	Garlic Powder
2 tsp	1 1/2 Tbsp	3 Tbsp	Ground Thyme

Directions:

- Using either bread loaves or leftover garlic bread, slice bread into ¼ inch pieces.
- Toss with oil, balsamic, thyme and garlic powder.
- Bake in a preheated oven at 400°F degrees for 45 minutes or until golden brown and crispy. Be sure to toss at least once during baking.
- Serve with Caesar Salad.

Bread Crumbs

Better to make more than you need because it really is a bummer when you run out and still have breading to do! Plus breadcrumbs freeze well for the next time you need them.

12 Servings	32 Servings	60 Servings	Ingredients
18 pieces	48 pieces	90 pieces	Left-Over Bread Ends or Slices
1 Tbsp	3 Tbsp	5 Tbsp	Oregano
2 tsp	1 Tbsp	3 Tbsp	Basil
1 Tbsp	3 Tbsp	5 Tbsp	Garlic Salt
1 Tbsp	3 Tbsp	5 Tbsp	Garlic Powder
¾ cup	2 cup	4 cups	Parmesan

Directions:

- Using a medium-sized bowl, save any leftover bread ends/pieces, garlic bread, hot dog buns, etc., and loosely cover the bowl to prevent any moisture getting in and turning the bread moldy. In other words, allow for some air flow to help the bread dry out.
- Once you have accumulated enough bread pieces, break bread into smaller pieces and blend in a food processor until small crumbs are formed.
- Store in a freezer bag and freeze until needed. Add spices and parmesan to breadcrumbs as needed and toss.

Basic Meat Sauce

Use this basic meat sauce for any dish that requires a meat sauce, such as Moussaka.

12 Servings	32 Servings	60 Servings	Ingredients
3 kg	8 kg	15 kg	Lean Ground Beef
2	5	8	Yellow Onions
3-4 Tbsp	6-8 Tbsp	15-16 Tbsp	Minced Garlic
1-1L	1-2.4 L	2-2.4 L	Diced Tomatoes
1-2.4 L	3-2.4 L	4-2.4 L	Tomato Sauce
2 Tbsp	4 Tbsp	6 Tbsp	Tomato Paste
2	3	5	Bay Leaves
¼ - ½ cup	¾ - 1 cup	1 ½ - 2 cups	Chicken Stock (to taste)
1 tsp	3 tsp	5 tsp	Red Pepper Flakes
2 Tbsp each	5 Tbsp each	7 Tbsp each	Italian Spices (Oregano, basil, thyme)
1 Tbsp	3 Tbsp	5 Tbsp	Cumin
1 Tbsp	3 Tbsp	5 Tbsp	BBQ Sauce
½ Tbsp	3 Tbsp	5 Tbsp	Lemon Juice
1 Tbsp	5 Tbsp	10 Tbsp	Worcestershire Sauce
1 Tbsp	3 Tbsp	5 Tbsp	Garlic Powder

Directions:

- In a large rondeau, heat oil and cook beef until fully cooked. I use a potato masher to break down any big clumps of beef, or once meat has been cooled break apart any meat clumps with your hands.
- Strain the meat until most of the grease is gone (reserve a bit of grease for flavor) and set aside.
- Peel garlic and onions. Mince garlic and finely dice onions.
- In a medium sauce pan, heat a couple of tablespoons of oil and sauté minced garlic and onions until the onions are translucent.
- Add garlic and onions to the meat, also add tomato sauce, diced tomatoes and juice and spices (bay leaves, oregano, basil and thyme, garlic powder,

chili pepper flakes, cumin and cinnamon) and begin simmering over low heat.

- Add chicken stock, BBQ sauce, Worcestershire sauce and lemon juice. Lemon juice will help cut down on any acidity from the tomatoes. Simmer for at least 1½ hours and let the flavors merge.

Non-Dairy Mushroom Cream Sauce

Makes a great alternative for those allergic to dairy or for vegans. And still tastes creamy!

12 Servings	32 Servings	60 Servings	Ingredients
1 Tbsp	3 Tbsp	5 Tbsp	Olive Oil
1	2	3	Onions
1 ¾ cups	4 ¾ cups	9 cups	Cooked Rice
3 ¾ cups	10 cups	18 ¾ cups	Beef or Vegetable Stock
1 ¼ cup	3 cups	5 cups	Brown Mushrooms
1 Tbsp	3 Tbsp	5 Tbsp	Dijon
1 ½ cups	4 cups	7 cups	White Wine Vinegar
1 tsp	½ Tbsp	1 Tbsp	Salt and Pepper
1 Tbsp	3 Tbsp	5 Tbsp	Tamari
1 Tbsp	3 Tbsp	5 Tbsp	Tarragon

Directions:

- Finely dice onions. Wash brown mushrooms and slice thinly.
- Using a large frying pan, heat oil and add finely diced onion. Sauté until soft. Add sliced brown mushrooms and cook until tender.
- Add half the amount of the white wine vinegar to the hot pan and deglaze and reduce until the liquid is half the amount.
- Stir in Dijon, tamari and salt and pepper to taste. In a large food processor, blend rice with the mushroom sauce until creamy and transfer to a large stock pot.
- Add beef broth to the mushroom sauce and the tarragon and simmer until the flavors merge. Adjust seasoning to taste. Serve over baked pork chops, chicken or stroganoff noodles.

Pizza Sauce

If you are ever in a pinch you can use prepared pizza sauce but it really takes no time at all to jazz up a can of crushed tomato sauce.

12 Servings	32 Servings	60 Servings	Ingredients
1 Tbsp	3 Tbsp	5 Tbsp	Olive Oil
2 - 540 ml	1 - 2.4 L	2 - 2.4 L	Canned Crushed Tomato Sauce
1 Tbsp	3 Tbsp	5 Tbsp	Oregano
1 Tbsp	3 Tbsp	5 Tbsp	Crushed Fresh Garlic
½ tsp	½ Tbsp	1Tbsp	Salt (or to taste)
½ Tsp	1 ½ Tbsp	3 Tbsp	Sugar

Directions:

- Combine olive oil, crushed tomato sauce, oregano, sugar and crushed garlic (I would use a garlic press to crush the garlic) and simmer over medium heat until the flavors merge.
- Left-over pizza sauce can be added to other savory Italian sauces or kept frozen for the next time.

Basic Tomato Sauce

A simple yet savory tomato sauce...

12 Servings	32 Servings	60 Servings	Ingredients
3 Tbsp	5 Tbsp	8 Tbsp	Olive Oil
1 2.4 L can	2 2.4 L cans	3 2.4 L cans	Crushed Tomatoes or Plum Tomatoes
3 Tbsp	5 Tbsp	8 Tbsp	Tomato Paste
1	2	3	Large Onion
5	12	20	Minced Garlic Cloves
½ Tbsp	2 Tbsp	3 Tbsp	Lemon Juice
1 Tbsp	2 Tbsp	3 Tbsp	Granulated Sugar
1 1/2 Tbsp	5Tbsp	7 Tbsp	Dried Basil
1 1/2 Tbsp	5 Tbsp	7 Tbsp	Oregano
1 1/2 Tbsp	5 Tbsp	7 Tbsp	Marjoram
1 Tbsp	3 Tbsp	5 Tbsp	Garlic Powder

Directions:

- Peel and finely mince onion. In a large stock pot add oil and heat over medium low heat. Add finely minced onion and sauté.
- Finely mince garlic and add to sautéing onions. Add marjoram, basil and oregano.
- Add either canned crushed tomatoes or plum tomatoes. If using plum tomatoes, puree the tomatoes with the above ingredients.
- Add tomato paste, lemon juice, sugar and garlic powder and let simmer until the flavors merge, stirring occasionally.

SALADS & SALAD DRESSINGS

■ Salads are a great addition to any meal and are a must for sound nutrition. Homemade salad dressings are easy and not loaded with preservatives and sugars like the store-bought variety. The best salads are made with fresh ingredients and lightly coated with a well-balanced vinaigrette. To help prevent your salad from wilting, toss lightly with olive oil. This will help the salad hold up better when tossed with a vinegar based dressing.

Vegetarian Cobb Salad

A savory salad with a Dijon vinaigrette that can be served with chopped bacon on the side.

12 Servings	32 Servings	60 Servings	Ingredients
12 cups	32 cups	60 cups	Spinach
2	5	10	Red Peppers
3	8	15	Hard Boiled Eggs
2	3	4	Red Onion
¾ cup	1 ½ cups	3 cups	Toasted Sunflower seeds, Pumpkin seeds or Slivered Almonds
2	4	8	Avocados
1 ½ cups	3 cups	6 cups	Shredded Mozzarella
¾ cup	1 ½ cups	3 cups	Diced Bacon

Dressing:

1 Tbsp	3 Tbsp	5 Tbsp	Dijon
1-2 cloves	2-3 cloves	3-4 cloves	Crushed Garlic (or to taste)
1 cup	2 ½ cups	4 cups	Grape Seed Oil or Olive Oil
½ cup	1 ½ cups	3 cups	Apple Cider Vinegar
1 ½ tsp	1 Tbsp	2 Tbsp	Honey or Agave Syrup
½ tsp	1 tsp	1 ½ tsp	Salt or to taste

Directions:

- Wash and dry spinach if it already hasn't already been washed prior to packaging.
- Place eggs in cold water, bring to a rolling boil and boil softly for about 15 minutes. Add 1 Tbsp of salt or vinegar to cold water to help peel the eggs. Remove immediately from hot water and place under cold water. Once cooled, peel and slice eggs using an egg slicer or a knife into 2 mm rounds and dice into bits.

- Use leftover bacon or cook bacon, fat side up, for about 45 minutes. Drain fat into an empty can (coffee tins work great for this) and let cool. Once cool, dice bacon into bite-size pieces.
- Shred mozzarella and set aside.
- Wash and then dice red pepper. Remove inner seeds and membrane.
- Peel and dice avocado and red onion.
- Toast sunflower seeds or almond slivers in oven at 350°F until golden brown. Make sure to set a timer because I can't tell you how many times I have forgotten about the seeds or nuts being toasted in the oven only to end up with them being burnt. Or you can toast them in a pan on a stove top for about 5 minutes. If you choose to toast in a pan do so over medium heat and watch continually as they can burn easily.
- Prepare dressing by peeling garlic. Use the side of your knife and press down and peel away the outer layer. Mince the garlic using a garlic press or sharp knife. Combine garlic with oil, vinegar, Dijon, honey and salt and mix. Adjust seasonings to taste.
- Toss all the ingredients together, except dressing. Add dressing just before serving, except the bacon. I set the bacon aside and let the guests add it themselves, in case there are any vegetarians. I add the dressing myself to the salads for convenience. However, if you want your guests to serve themselves then make a double batch of the dressing and put it in a squeeze bottle with the top cut off for easy pouring.

Citrus Asian Salad

This is a simple yet delightful Asian inspired salad that hits the spot on a hot day.

12 Servings	32 Servings	60 Servings	Ingredients
2 heads	6-7 heads	12-13 heads	Romaine Lettuce
1 small can	3 small cans	5 small cans	Mandarin Oranges and Juice (reserve juice for dressing)
6	12	20	Diced Scallions
3	5	8	Cucumbers
2	4	7	Avocados
2 cups	3 Cups	4 Cups	Asian Stir Fry Noodles
1 Tbsp	2 Tbsp	4 Tbsp	Sesame Seeds

Dressing:

12 Servings	32 Servings	60 Servings	Ingredients
3 Tbsp	5 Tbsp	8 Tbsp	Sesame Oil
½ cup	1 cup	2 cup	Grapeseed Oil
¼ cup	½ cup	1 cup	Rice Wine Vinegar
1 Tbsp	3 Tbsp	5 Tbsp	Minced Ginger
1 Tbsp	3 Tbsp	5 Tbsp	Minced Garlic
1 tsp	1 ½ tsp	2 tsp	Pepper (or to taste)
3 Tbsp	5 Tbsp	¼ cup	Soya Sauce
1 tsp	1 Tbsp	2 Tbsp	Honey
			*Salt to Taste
			*Juice from Mandarin Oranges

Directions:

- Mince garlic and ginger.
- Prepare dressing by combining sesame oil and grapeseed oil, rice vinegar, juice from mandarins, soya sauce, salt, pepper, crushed garlic and minced ginger.
- Chop romaine lettuce into bite-sized pieces, wash in a salad spinner and dry.

- Dice scallions on an angle.
- Dice avocado and cucumbers. If preparing in advance then soak avocado lightly in lemon juice to prevent it from turning brown or grey.
- In a large bowl, mix together lettuce, cucumbers, scallions and avocado. Add mandarin oranges right before serving and toss with dressing.
- Sprinkle Asian noodles and sesame seeds on top before serving.

Greek Salad

Add diced romaine lettuce to help extend a traditional Greek salad.

12 Servings	32 Servings	60 Servings	Ingredients
1	5	8	Red Peppers
1	6	8	Green Peppers
1	6	8	Yellow or Orange Peppers
1	4	6	Cucumbers
2	5	10	Ripe Tomatoes
1	4	6	Red Onions
2-3 heads	5-6 heads	7-8 heads	Romaine Lettuce
1 ½ cup	3 cups	5 cups	Feta
1 cup	2 cups	3 cups	Black Pitted Olives

Dressing:

¼ cup	¾ cup	2 cups	Red Wine Vinegar
¼ cup	¾ cup	2 cups	Balsamic Vinegar
2 tsp	2 Tbsp	3 Tbsp	Dijon Mustard
2-3 cloves	4-5 cloves	6-7 cloves	Crushed Garlic
½ cup	1 cup	2 cups	Olive Oil
1 Tbsp	3 Tbsp	5 Tbsp	Oregano
1 ½ tsp	1 Tbsp	2 Tbsp	Honey or Agave Syrup
1 ½ tsp	1 Tbsp	2 Tbsp	Crushed Fennel seeds or Tarragon
1 tsp	2 tsp	1 Tbsp	Sea Salt

Directions:

- Wash peppers, tomatoes, cucumbers and dice into medium-sized pieces.
- Dice onions into medium-sized pieces.
- Slice romaine into bite-sized pieces, wash in a salad spinner and spin dry.

- Prepare dressing by combining minced garlic, vinegars, oil, oregano, salt, Dijon and sweetener. Add tarragon or if using fennel, crush seeds in a mortar and pestle and add to dressing.
- Combine veggies, onions, feta and olives.
- Toss above ingredients, except romaine and feta, with dressing and marinate for about ½ hour. Add lettuce and feta just before serving.

Creamy Sundried Tomato & Roasted Red Pepper Bowtie Pasta Salad

Loaded with yummy Sundried Tomatoes. For a healthier option, try substituting whole wheat pasta.

12 Servings	32 Servings	60 Servings	Ingredients
¾ cup	1 ½ cups	2 cups	Sundried Tomatoes
3 Tbsp	8 Tbsp	1 cup	Clubhouse Roasted Red Pepper & Garlic Seasoning
¼ cup	¾ cup	1 ¼ cup	Olive Oil
2	4	6	Red Peppers
1	2	3	Red Onions
6 cups	16 cups	30 cups	Bowtie Pasta

Dressing:

12 Servings	32 Servings	60 Servings	Ingredients
2 cups	5 cups	8 cups	Mayo or Miracle Whip
1 ½ tsp	1 ½ Tbsp	3 Tbsp	Agave Sweetener (only if using real mayo)
½ Tbsp	1 Tbsp	2 Tbsp	Sea Salt
1 Tbsp	3 Tbsp	5 Tbsp	Pepper

Directions:

- In a large stock pot bring water to a boil. Once boiling, add half the salt to the water just before adding the pasta. Also, add 1 Tbsp of oil to water to prevent the noodles from sticking together. Boil noodles until just about tender (better to be al dente). Noodles are finished cooking when the edges of the pasta turn white or in the case of brown noodles a lighter color than the rest of the pasta. Cook the noodles for about 15 minutes at a rolling boil.
- Drain and rinse under cold water and let cool. Toss in olive oil to prevent the noodles from sticking even further. Quick tip: if you need the pasta to cool quickly, place pasta in a bowl and then place in freezer until it has cooled down to a reasonable temperature. Make sure not to forget about it!

- Using a food processor, blend sundried tomatoes, clubhouse seasoning and oil together. It is important to do this step first to help the dehydrated pieces of red pepper and garlic in the seasoning to become reconstituted. Then add the mayo, sugar (only if using real mayonnaise), salt and pepper together. Add a bit of milk or more oil if the dressing is too thick.
- If you cannot find the clubhouse seasoning you can substitute a roasted red pepper and roasted garlic bulb. Simply drizzle the red pepper and garlic bulb with olive oil and roast for 40 -50 minutes at 350 F. Let cool and peel the skin from the red pepper and roasted garlic. Add red pepper and a few garlic cloves at a time to the food processor, tasting as you go. You may need to adjust the amount of salt.
- Finely dice red pepper and red onion. Mix cooled pasta with veggies and salad dressing and serve.
- This salad will keep till the next day but you may need to add a little extra dressing as the pasta will soak up the dressing.

Spinach & Strawberries with Poppyseed Dressing

A delightful salad with toasted pecans or walnuts sweetened with agave syrup.

12 Servings	32 Servings	60 Servings	Ingredients
3 cups	6 cups	10 cups	Sliced Strawberries
2	3	4	Red Onions
1 ½ cups	3 cups	5 cups	Sweetened Pecans or Walnuts
12 Cups	1 Kg	1 ½ Kg	Spinach (estimate about 3/4 cup of spinach for each person)

Dressing:

¾ cup	2 ¼ cups	4 cups	Olive oil
½ cup	1 ½ cup	3 cups	Wine Vinegar or Apple Cider Vinegar
2 tsp	1-2 Tbsp	3-4 Tbsp	Dijon Mustard
2 Tbsp	4 Tbsp	6 Tbsp	Honey or Agave Syrup
2 Tbsp	6 Tbsp	12 Tbsp	Poppy Seeds
½ tsp	1 tsp	1 ½ tsp	Sea Salt (or to taste)

Directions:

- Measure olive oil and vinegar into a large juice jug pitcher and blend with Dijon mustard, half of the honey and salt. Mix in poppy seeds.
- Wash strawberries and slice thinly lengthwise.
- Peel and julienne the red onion.
- Roast pecans or walnuts in either a frying pan over medium low heat or in the oven at 325°F. Add the remainder of the honey or agave syrup just before the nuts are finished cooking and toss.
- Just before serving, pour the dressing over the salad and serve immediately. You will find that this salad shrinks considerable as the spinach wilts from the acidity of the vinegar. As mentioned above it is a good idea to harden off the spinach by tossing lightly in oil prior to service.

Option: Try adding soft goat cheese or feta.

Roasted Garlic Caesar Salad

Add balsamic croutons for a different twist on a traditional salad.

12 Servings	32 Servings	60 Servings	Ingredients
2 heads	5 -7 heads	10 -12 heads	Romaine
1/2 cup	1 cup	2 cups	Bacon Bits
1 cup	3 cups	5 cups	Croutons

Dressing:

12 Servings	32 Servings	60 Servings	Ingredients
2	5	12	Egg Yolks (or substitute 1 Tbsp mayonnaise for each egg)
3 Tbsp	8 Tbsp	15 Tbsp	Lemon Juice (fresh or concentrate)
2 Tbsp	5 Tbsp	10 Tbsp	Red Wine Vinegar
5-6 cloves	1 whole bulb	2 whole bulbs	Roasted Garlic
1 ½ tsp	1 ½ Tbsp	2 Tbsp	Anchovy Paste
1 Tbsp	2 Tbsp	4 Tbsp	Capers
2 tsp	4 tsp	6 tsp	Cracked Black Pepper (or to taste)
1 Tbsp	2 Tbsp	4 Tbsp	Worcestershire Sauce
1 ½ cups	4 cups	10 cups	Olive Oil
1 cup	2 cups	4 cups	Parmesan
1 Tbsp	3 Tbsp	5 Tbsp	Dijon Mustard
			*Salt to taste

Directions:

- With the peel on, roast garlic in a pan drizzled with olive oil on top for approximately 20 minutes.
- Remove garlic from peel and, using a plastic juice jug, combine garlic with lemon juice, red wine vinegar, capers, anchovies and cracked pepper.
- Add shredded parmesan cheese and slowly add olive oil, pulsing with a hand blender until mixed.
- Pour over romaine and serve with shaved parmesan and balsamic roasted croutons.

Omit anchovy paste if serving vegetarians.

Broccoli Buffet Salad

This broccoli-savvy salad is sure to please even the pickiest palates.

12 Servings	32 Servings	60 Servings	Ingredients
7-8 (12 Cups)	18-20 (32 Cups)	45-48 (60 cups)	Broccoli Crowns
1 ½ cups	3 cups	5 cups	Cheddar Cheese (cubed)
¾ cup	1 ½ cups	3 cups	Dried Cranberries
1	2	3	Red Onions
¾ cup	1 ½ cups	3 cups	Sunflower Seeds

Dressing:

12 Servings	32 Servings	60 Servings	Ingredients
3 Cups	7 Cups	12 Cups	Plain Yogurt
1/2 Cup	1 Cup	2 Cups	Red Wine Vinegar
2 Tbsp	5 Tbsp	7 Tbsp	Sweetener , to taste (Sugar, Agave Syrup, Honey)
1 tsp	½ Tbsp	1 Tbsp	Cracked Pepper (or to taste)
½ Tbsp	1 Tbsp	1 ½ Tbsp	Sea Salt (or to taste)
1 Tbsp	2 Tbsp	4 Tbsp	Worcestershire sauce
2 Tbsp	4 Tbsp	10 Tbsp	Lemon Juice

Vegan Dressing:

12 Servings	32 Servings	60 Servings	Ingredients
½ 350 g	1 350 g	1 ½ 350 g	Soft Silken Tofu
¼ Cup	¾ cup	1 ½ cups	Apple Cider Vinegar
3 Tbsp	¼ cup	1 cup	Red Wine Vinegar
1 Cup	2 cups	4 cups	Soy Milk
3 Tbsp	¼ cup	1 cup	Olive Oil
1 Tbsp	3 Tbsp	5 Tbsp	Sweetener (Agave, Honey or Cane Sugar)
2 tsp	1 Tbsp	3 Tbsp	Dijon Mustard
1 tsp	½ Tbsp	1 Tbsp	Cracked Pepper (or to taste)
1 tsp	½ Tbsp	1 Tbsp	Sea Salt (or taste)
1 ½ Tbsp	3 Tbsp	5 Tbsp	Worcestershire Sauce

Directions:

- If not using broccoli crowns, cut the stems off the broccoli and discard. Break broccoli heads into small pieces and wash.
- Dice cheddar cheese into ¼ inch cubes.
- Peel and julienne red onion.
- Combine dressing ingredients together and pour over broccoli. Mix in the remaining ingredients. Best if the salad can rest for half an hour before serving so the broccoli can soak up some of the dressing.
- If making the vegan version, omit cheddar cheese.

Mediterranean Orzo Salad

A nice twist on a traditional Greek salad.

12 Servings	32 Servings	60 Servings	Ingredients
3 cups	8 cups	12 cups	Orzo
12 cups	1 kg	1 ½ kg	Spinach
1 ½ cups	3 cups	5 cups	Pitted Black Olives
1 cup	3 cups	5 cups	Feta
1	3	5	Red Peppers
1	3	5	Green Peppers
1	3	5	Yellow Peppers
1	3	5	Orange Peppers
1	2	3	Red Onions

Dressing:

1 ½ tsp	1/2 Tbsp	2 Tbsp	Fennel Seeds
¾ cup	1½ cups	3 cups	Balsamic Oil
1 cup	2 cups	5 cups	Olive Oil or Grape Seed Oil
2 tsp	2 Tbsp	3 Tbsp	Dijon
1 Tbsp	3 Tbsp	5 Tbsp	Agave Syrup or Honey
½ tsp	1 tsp	1½ tsp	Sea Salt

Directions:

- Boil orzo noodles according to the package instructions and let cool.
- Wash and dice peppers.
- Peel and dice onions.
- Add spinach, olives, feta and orzo pasta.
- Using a hand held blender, blend balsamic, olive oil, Dijon, salt and agave syrup. Crush fennel in a mortar and pestle and add to dressing.
- Add as much dressing as needed just prior to serving. It is important to not coat the salad with dressing, and remember that larger serving sizes will require two bowls, so save half of the dressing for the second bowl of salad.

Mixed Greens with Shredded Beets and Carrots & Agave Sweetened Pumpkin Seeds

A healthy and simple yet satisfying salad.

12 Servings	32 Servings	60 Servings	Ingredients
2 heads	6-7 heads	10-11 heads	Red Leaf Lettuce, Butter Lettuce or Mixed Greens
1 large	2 large	3 large	Beets
2 large	3 large	4 large	Carrots
3-4 stalks	5-6 stalks	7-8 stalks	Green Onion
¾ cup	1 ½ cups	3 cups	Roasted Pumpkin Seeds
½ Tbsp	1 ½ Tbsp	2 Tbsp	Agave Syrup

Dressing:

¾ cup	1 ½ cup	3 ½ cups	Balsamic or Apple Cider Vinegar
1 cup	2 cups	4 cups	Olive Oil
1 ½ tsp	3 tsp	6 tsp	Agave Syrup (or to taste)
½ tsp	¾ tsp	1 tsp	Sea Salt
1 ½ tsp	3 tsp	6 tsp	Fresh Dill (optional)

Directions:

- Using a serrated knife, chop lettuce and wash in a salad spinner. Peel and shred beets and carrots and finely dice green onions.
- Heat pumpkin seeds in a pan until lightly browned and add agave syrup to the seeds just before they are finished browning. Remove from hot pan and place in a bowl to cool before adding to salad. The sugar will cause the pumpkin seeds to stick together, so you will have to break the seeds apart into smaller pieces.
- Using a hand blender, mix dressing ingredients together. If using dill, finely chop dill and add to dressing.
- Pour over salad just before serving. Voilà, a delicious, healthy meal!

Dijon Potato Salad with Artichokes

Not your boring potato salad.

12 Servings	32 Servings	60 Servings	Ingredients
12-15	32-35	60-63	Red Potatoes or New Potatoes
2-3 stalks	5-7 stalks	1 bunch	Celery
5-6 hearts	1 - 540 ml can	2 - 540 ml cans	Artichoke Hearts (reserve the juice for the dressing)
1	1 ½	2	Red Onions
3 Tbsp	5 Tbsp	7 Tbsp	Fresh Parsley

Dressing:

12 Servings	32 Servings	60 Servings	Ingredients
1 Tbsp	3 Tbsp	5 Tbsp	Dijon Mustard
2 Tbsp	5 Tbsp	¾ cup	Artichoke Juice
3 cups	7 cups	12 cups	Mayo or Miracle Whip
1 Tbsp	2 Tbsp	3 Tbsp	Lemon Juice
1 Tbsp	1 ½ Tbsp	2 Tbsp	Worcestershire Sauce
1 Tbsp	3 Tbsp	5 Tbsp	Sweetner (Honey, Sugar or Agave Syrup)
1 Tbsp	1 ½ Tbsp	2 Tbsp	Sea Salt (or to taste)
1 tsp	2 tsp	1 Tbsp	Pepper (or to taste
1 ½ tsp	2 tsp	3 tsp	Celery seed
1 Tbsp	3 Tbsp	5 Tbsp	Fresh Dill

Option: Add a touch of milk to the dressing if you find it too thick.

Directions:

- Wash and rinse potatoes, but do not remove the skin. The skin has all the flavor and most of the nutrients. Depending on the size of the potato quarter or halve the potatoes and place in cold water to prevent them from turning grey. In a medium- to large-sized pot, add potatoes to cold water and bring to a boil in salted water until just about soft but not mushy. Quick tip: To test doneness, using a fork, stick the fork through the potato, and if the potato falls off the fork right away it is done.

- Strain potatoes immediately (otherwise they will keep cooking in the pot) and let cool.
- Wash and dice celery into small pieces.
- Peel and dice finely the red onion.
- Remove artichokes from juice and chop. Don't discard the juice from the artichokes because you can use it in the dressing.
- Wash and mince fresh parsley.
- To make dressing, using a blender, add all the ingredients together except the celery seed and pulse until mixed.
- Pour over potatoes and let sit for an hour before service so the potatoes can soak up some of the flavor from the dressing. Taste before serving and adjust the flavours as needed.

Couscous Salad with Dried Fruit

A Moroccan favorite sure to satisfy any taste buds.

12 Servings	32 Servings	60 Servings	Ingredients
3 cups	8 cups	15 cups	Couscous
6 cups	16 cups	30 cups	Water
1 Tbsp	3 Tbsp	5 Tbsp	Chicken or Vegetarian Stock
1 cup	1 ½ cups	2 cups	Dried Currants, Apricots or Raisons
½ cup	1 ½ cups	2 cups	Sliced Almonds
2-3 stalks	6-7 stalks	7-8 stalks	Green Onions
1	2	3	Red peppers
1	2	3	Cucumbers
1	2	3	Tomatoes
1 cup	2 cups	3 cups	Chick Peas (rinsed)
3 Tbsp	8 Tbsp	1 cup	Minced Fresh Parsley or Mint
2 Tsp	2 Tbsp	3 Tbsp	Cinnamon
1 ½ tsp	2 Tbsp	3 Tbsp	Ground Ginger
1 ½ tsp	3 Tbsp	4 Tbsp	Cumin
1 tsp	1 Tbsp	2 Tbsp	Turmeric
3 Tbsp	½ cup	1 cup	Lemon Juice
¼ cup	¾ cup	1 ½ cups	Olive oil
4 cloves	6 cloves	8 cloves	Minced Garlic
1 ½ tsp	1 Tbsp	1 ½ Tbsp	Salt (or to taste)
1 tsp	2 tsp	1 Tbsp	Freshly Ground Pepper (or to taste

Directions:

- In a large stock pot, bring water, chicken or vegetarian stock and couscous to a boil. Boil until all the water has been soaked up by the couscous. Fluff with a fork and allow couscous to cool. Keep stirring throughout the cooling process.

- If using apricots chop into small pieces or process in a food processor. Quick Tip: Use a wet knife for easier chopping of dried fruits and nuts.
- Wash all the veggies.
- Mince green onion, and dice peppers and cucumber into ¼ inch pieces. Peel garlic and mince into small pieces.
- Measure spices into a bowl and mix together before adding to couscous.
- Mix couscous, veggies, garlic, dried fruit, spices, lemon juice and olive oil. Add minced parsley or mint.

Thai Vermicelli Noodle Salad

A delicious Thai-inspired dish that is so easy to prepare.

12 Servings	32 Servings	60 Servings	Ingredients
454 g	900 g	1400 g	Vermicelli Rice Noodles
2	5	10	Julienned Carrot
2	5	10	Diced Red Pepper
3 sprigs	8 sprigs	15 sprigs	Green Onion
¾ cup	2 cups	3 ¾ cups	Roasted Peanuts
3 Tbsp	8 Tbsp	¾ cup	Minced Cilantro
¼ cup	1 ½ cups	3 cups	Fresh Mango or Papaya

Dressing:

12 Servings	32 Servings	60 Servings	Ingredients
½ cup	1 cup	2 cups	Thai Sweet & Hot Sauce
1/2 cup	1 ½ cups	2 ½ cups	Smooth Peanut Butter
¼ cup	1 cup	1 ½ cups	Rice Wine Vinegar
1/4 cup	1 cup	2 cups	Sesame Oil
3 Tbsp	¼ cup	½ cup	Braggs, Tamari or Soya Sauce
2	6	12	Fresh Limes
1 Tbsp	3 Tbsp	5 Tbsp	Fish Sauce
			*Sea Salt to taste

Directions:

- Boil enough hot water to cover the noodles, about 4 cups for each package of noodles. Place noodles in a large bowl and pour hot water over noodles and let sit until soft, about 20 minutes. Strain and cool in very cold water to prevent the noodles from sticking together.
- Peel and julienne the carrots. Wash and dice red pepper and green onion diagonally.

- Roast peanuts at 350°F for 20 minutes or until slightly browned, or simply buy roasted peanuts. Once cooled, mince roasted peanuts with a knife, or pulse in a food processor.
- Wash and finely chop fresh cilantro.
- Combine the dressing ingredients and mix. Add sea salt at the end only if it needs it. A note about fish sauce: I always add a teaspoon to a tablespoon at a time, depending on the amount, because of the saltiness of fish sauce, and then I add more if the dish needs it. It is a very powerful ingredient! Adjust seasoning to taste.
- Strain noodles and blot with a paper towel to soak up any excess water. Mix dressing with noodles and toss with cilantro, carrots, green onion and carrots. Adjust flavours to taste. Sprinkle peanuts over top.

Thai Quinoa Salad

A favorite of mine and packed full of protein from the quinoa.

12 Servings	32 Servings	60 Servings	Ingredients
3 cups	8 cups	15 cups	Quinoa
4 ½ cups	12 cups	22 ½ cups	Water
1 Tbsp	3 Tbsp	5 Tbsp	Chicken or Vegetable Stock
2	5	7	Carrots
2	5	7	Cucumbers
2	5	7	Red Peppers
3 Tbsp	8 Tbsp	1 cup	Fresh Cilantro
3 Tbsp	8 Tbsp	1 cup	Sweet Thai Basil
1	2	3	Red Onions
2	4	6	Mangoes
1	3	6	Avocados
2	5	7	Garlic Cloves
3 Tbsp	5 Tbsp	8 Tbsp	Lime Juice (fresh or from concentrate)
½ tsp	2 tsp	1 Tbsp	Pepper (or to taste)
2 Tbsp	¼ cup	1 cup	Thai Sweet Chili Sauce
1 Tbsp	2 Tbsp	4 Tbsp	Powdered Lemon Grass (optional)
1/2 tsp	1 1/2 tsp	2 tsp	Sea Salt (or to taste)
1 Tbsp	¼ cup	¾ cup	Olive Oil

Directions:

- Rinse quinoa under cold water. This step is really important otherwise the quinoa will taste bitter.
- In a medium-sized pot, bring water, stock and quinoa to a boil and let simmer until the quinoa has soaked up all the stock. Let stand for 5 minutes, then fluff with a fork and let cool.
- Peel and julienne carrots. Also wash and finely dice cucumber and peppers.

- Peel and dice garlic, onion, and mango.
- Peel avocado and remove the pit by either scooping it out or sticking the edge of your knife into the pit and pull it out from the middle. Scoop out the avocado from the rind and cut lengthwise down the avocado and then across the other way.
- Toss the above ingredients together.
- Wash and finely mince fresh herbs.
- Add lime juice, salt, Thai sauce and herbs. Toss until well mixed.

SOUPS

■ The best soups are made with a homemade chicken or vegetable stock. When I cook for a large crowd, I usually make a vegetarian stock rather than a chicken stock. Then I don't have to make two soups. Making a soup stock is simple and easy to use.

Homemade Soup Stock

I don't really have a quantity laid out for this recipe as it really depends on what ingredients you have on hand. I save all of my vegetable peels including:

- Onions
- Carrots
- Leeks
- Turnips
- Beets
- Garlic
- Yams
- Sweet Potatoes
- Celery ribs and leaves

Then I add water until just above the vegetable peels and include a bouquet garni of dried spices. I find cheese cloth works best for this. Include in this:

- 1 Tbsp of Marjoram
- ½ Tbsp Dried Sage
- 2 Bay leaves (lightly crushed)
- 1 Tbsp dried Thyme
- 1 Tbsp Dried Parsley
- 2 Garlic Cloves

Vegetable Chowder

A nice savory soup.

12 Servings	32 Servings	60 Servings	Ingredients
3 Tbsp	4 Tbsp	6 Tbsp	Oil
2	3	4	Onion
6 cloves	12 cloves	22 cloves	Garlic
3 cups	8 cups	15 cups	Red Potato
4 cups	9 cups	18 cups	Turnips
¾ cups	2 cups	4 cups	Diced Carrots
2 cups	5 cups	10 cups	Corn
1 ½ cups	3 cups	5 cups	Fennel bulbs
2 cups	5 cups	8 cups	Chopped Tomatoes
9 cups	24 cups	35 cups	Milk
9 cups	24 cups	35 cups	Water or Homemade Soup Stock
3 Tbsp	9 Tbsp	1 cup	Dry Vegetable or Chicken Bouillon Base (or to taste)
1 Tbsp	3 Tbsp	5 Tbsp	Thyme
1 Tbsp	3 Tbsp	5 Tbsp	Basil
1 Tbsp	3 Tbsp	5 Tbsp	Oregano
1 Tbsp	3 Tbsp	5 Tbsp	Sea Salt (or to taste)
1 Tbsp	2 Tbsp	3 Tbsp	Pepper (or to taste)
1 Tbsp	3 Tbsp	5 Tbsp	Fresh Parsley
2	4	6	Bay Leaves

Directions:

- Peel both garlic and onions. Mince garlic finely and dice onions into medium-sized pieces. In a medium large stock pot, sauté onions on medium heat until they are translucent, then add garlic.
- Peel carrots and turnips and wash potatoes thoroughly. Dice potatoes, turnips, carrots and tomatoes (can substitute canned tomatoes for fresh) into medium-sized pieces.

- Remove the top part of the fennel and save the anise herb for seasoning. Discard the stems. Slice fennel bulb in half. Remove outer skin and slice again length wise in long skinny strips and mince.
- Add diced potatoes, turnips, carrots and fennel (but not corn and tomatoes) to the stock pot and sauté with garlic and onions until just about soft. Add the seasonings too, except the bay leaves, parsley and anise.
- Mince parsley and anise.
- Add either the water or homemade soup stock and milk to the sauteing vegetables. Add powdered bouillon base.
- Add corn and tomatoes and simmer until veggies are soft enough to purée with a blender.
- Add bay leaves, parsley and anise. Adjust seasonings to taste and let simmer until the flavors merge.

Pumpkin & Black Bean Soup

A delicious and satisfying soup made with Indian spices that will warm your soul. Use Coconut Milk for a rich creamy taste, or substitute water if you don't have any coconut milk on hand.

12 Servings	32 Servings	60 Servings	Ingredients
2 Tbsp	5 Tbsp	8 Tbsp	Oil (Canola/Vegetable, Clarified Butter or Ghee, Olive Oil or Grapeseed Oil)
2 - 796 ml cans	6 - 796 ml cans	12 - 796 ml	Pureed Pumpkin (non-spiced)
1 - 540 ml can	2 - 540 ml cans	3 - 540 ml cans	Black Beans
1 - 540 ml can	2 - 540 ml cans	3 - 540 ml cans	Diced Tomatoes
2	3	4	Onions
2-3 cloves	3-4 cloves	4-5 cloves	Garlic
2 Tbsp	5 Tbsp	8 Tbsp	Ginger
3 Tbsp	8 Tbsp	3/4 cup	Dry Chicken or Vegetable Bouillon Base (or to taste)
6 cups	16 cups	30 cups	Coconut Milk, Water or Homemade Soup Stock
2-3 Tbsp	½ cup	¾ cup	Maple Syrup or Honey (or to taste)
1 Tbsp	3 Tbsp	5 Tbsp	Coriander (fresh or ground)
1 Tbsp	3 Tbsp	5 Tbsp	Cumin
1 Tbsp	3 Tbsp	5 Tbsp	Mild Curry Paste or Powder
1 Tbsp	3 Tbsp	5 Tbsp	Turmeric
1 Tbsp	3 Tbsp	5 Tbsp	Cinnamon
2	3	5	Bay Leaves
1 Tbsp	2 Tbsp	3 Tbsp	Sea Salt (or to taste)

Directions:

- Peel and mince onions, ginger and garlic. In a large stock pot, heat oil over medium low heat. You can use clarified butter, peanut oil (if no peanut allergies) or vegetable oil. Sauté onions, garlic and ginger until the onions begin to turn translucent.
- After the onions begin to turn translucent, add curry paste, turmeric, cumin, cinnamon and coriander if using ground coriander.
- If using coconut milk, add the thick milk formed at the top of the can by scooping it from the top. Works best if you do not shake the can prior to use. Reserve the coconut water. Substitute with water or homemade soup stock if not using coconut milk.
- Mix the coconut milk you scooped off from the top of the coconut water in with the onions, garlic, ginger and spices. Let coconut milk bring out the oils from the curry paste before you add any other ingredients. This will help produce robust flavors.
- Add the puréed pumpkin and rinsed black beans and mix together.
- Once all the flavors have been incorporated together, then add the rest of the coconut water and dry bouillon base.
- Add canned diced tomatoes and juice.
- Add the bay leaves.
- If using fresh coriander, rinse and mince, and add to soup just before serving.
- Add salt if desired and adjust seasonings to taste. Simmer and let the flavors merge.

Barley Borscht

Use canned beets to save time, and add lots of fresh dill for a punch of flavor.

12 Servings	32 Servings	60 Servings	Ingredients
3 Tbsp	6 Tbsp	9 Tbsp	Butter or non-hydrogenated margarine
3 cups	8 cups	15 cups	Diced Onions
2 -3 cloves	3-4 cloves	5-6 cloves	Garlic
3 cups	8 cups	15 cups	Cabbage (finely shredded)
1 ½ cups	4 cups	7 cups	Diced Carrots
1 ½ cups	4 cups	7 cups	Diced Celery
3 1L	5 1L – 348	8 1L – 348	Canned Beets (including juice)
3 Tbsp	8 Tbsp	¾ cup	Dry Chicken or Vegetable Bouillon Base (or to taste)
12 cups	32 cups	60 cups	Water or Homemade Soup Stock
2 Tbsp	4 Tbsp	8 Tbsp	Red Wine Vinegar/ Apple Cider Vinegar
3 Tbsp	8 Tbsp	15 Tbsp	Fresh Dill
1 Tbsp	3 Tbsp	5 Tbsp	Dill Seed
¾ cup	2 cups	4 cups	Barley
2	3	5	Bay Leaves
½ Tbsp	2 Tbsp	3 Tbsp	Sea Salt (or to taste)
½ Tbsp	2 Tbsp	3 Tbsp	Pepper (or to taste)

Directions:

- Using a strainer, rinse barley first until barley runs clear. To reduce cooking time, soak barley overnight. Using 2 ½ cups of water to every cup of barley, bring water to a boil. If using soaked barley, add barley to boiling salted water and boil for twenty minutes, otherwise cook the barley for 40 minutes. Set aside and let cool.

- Peel and mince garlic. Peel and dice onions and carrots into small pieces. Wash and dice celery into small cubes. Do not discard celery leaf, chop finely. Set ingredients aside.
- In a large stock pot, over medium heat sauté garlic, onions, carrots and celery in butter or oil until soft. Add dill seed and sauté to release the flavors.
- Once vegetables have softened, add all the juice from canned beets. Chop beets into small, bite-sized pieces and add to soup.
- Add vinegar, sea salt and pepper to taste
- Add either homemade vegetable stock or mix the chicken or vegetable bouillon base with water and add to soup. If using homemade soup stock, you still might want to add the dried stock to the soup for added flavor.
- Add fresh chopped dill and bay leaves.
- Let the flavors merge and adjust seasoning as necessary.
- Add cooked barley to the borscht just before serving.

Option: For a traditional taste add a dollop of sour cream on top of the soup.

Tom Yum Soup with Coconut Milk

A traditional Thai soup that can be made with or without coconut milk. Just ask your local Asian supermarket for Tom Yum paste. The overall flavors of this dish are sweet, salty, spicy and sour.

12 Servings	32 Servings	60 Servings	Ingredients
4 Tbsp	1 cup	2 cups	Tom Yum Paste (available at any Asian grocery store)
4 Tbsp	1/2 cup	3/4 cup	Coconut Oil
2	3	4	Onions
7-8	10-11	12-14	Thin Ginger Coins
3	6	9	Carrots
2 cups	3 cups	4 cups	Mushrooms (brown or white)
2	3	4	Red pepper
2 cups	3 cups	4 cups	Fresh Tomatoes (diced)
3 - 398 ml	8 - 398 ml	15 - 398 ml	Canned Coconut Milk
1 ½ cups	4 cups	7 cups	Water
2-3 Tbsp	5-7 Tbsp	9-11 Tbsp	Fish Sauce
1 Tbsp	3 Tbsp	5 Tbsp	Tamarind Sauce/Paste
3-4 pieces	5-6 pieces	9-10 pieces	Lemon Grass
4	6	8	Kaffir Lime Leaves
2 Tbsp	4 Tbsp	8 Tbsp	Sweet Basil Leaves or Cilantro

Can substitute all water for coconut milk.

Directions:

- Peel and dice onion into medium-sized chunks and set aside.
- Peel and slice carrots diagonally.
- Slice ginger into thin coins (leave skin on but make sure to wash first).
- Wash and julienne the red pepper.

- Wash mushrooms and cut into quarters.
- Cut the tops of off the lemon grass, cut into 2 inch long pieces and then slice the pieces in half lengthwise; peel the outer layer off and discard.
- In a lage stock pot, over medium low heat melt coconut oil and sauté onions, carrots, lemon grass and ginger until onions are soft, then add tom yum paste and fish sauce and sauté a few more minutes.

Tip: Fish sauce is a very strong ingredient, so start off with a little and add more as needed.

- Add coconut milk only (leave the coconut water until the very end). Sauté until the oil from the tom yum paste starts to show through the coconut milk.
- Then add the coconut water and the mushrooms, red pepper and tamarind sauce.
- Crush the kaffir lime leaves and add to soup. Add salt to taste if you desire, as well as cane sugar. Let simmer until flavors merge. Add tomatoes and minced basil or coriander right before serving.

Potato Leek Soup

Simple ingredients. Loads of flavor.

12 Servings	32 Servings	60 Servings	Ingredients
8 -10	20 - 22	32 - 33	Leeks
8	20	30	Red or all-purpose Potatoes
4-5 cloves	9-10 cloves	12-13 cloves	Garlic
2 Tbsp	4 Tbsp	6 Tbsp	Butter or Olive oil for vegans
6 cups	15 cups	30 cups	Half & Half Cream, Buttermilk or Regular Milk
3 cups	12 cups	18 cups	Water or Homemade soup stock
3 Tbsp	¼ cup	½ cup	Dry Chicken or Vegetable Bouillon Base (or to taste)
2	3	4	Bay leaves
1 Tbsp	2 Tbsp	3 Tbsp	Rosemary
1 ½ tsp	1 Tbsp	1 ½ Tbsp	Pepper (or to taste)
1 Tbsp	2 Tbsp	3 Tbsp	Sea Salt (or to taste)

Directions:

- Wash and dice potatoes into small pieces. Leave the skin of the potato on as it contains all of the nutrients. In a large stock pot, place diced potatoes in cold salted water and bring to a boil. Boil until potatoes are soft. Drain and set aside until cool.
- Prepare leeks by removing the top half of the stalk. Save the top half for soup stock or discard. Slice lengthwise and remove outside layers. Rinse under cold water to remove any dirt. Dice into small pieces.
- In medium to large frying pan, melt butter in pan and sauté leeks until tender. Add minced garlic and rosemary and sauté a few minutes longer.
- Purée potatoes with a hand blender. Add leeks, minced garlic and rosemary and stir.
- Add homemade soup stock or water and cream or milk. Season with bouillon base, salt and pepper to taste, and bay leaves.
- Adjust the seasoning and let simmer until the flavors merge. Be careful to not boil any cream soups as they will curdle if they are boiled.

Thai Green Coconut Soup

Green curry ranks in the middle in terms of hotness, yellow curry is most mild, and red is the hottest. This dish can be served as either a soup or main dish.

12 Servings	32 Servings	60 Servings	Ingredients
2 Tbsp	3 Tbsp	4 Tbsp	Coconut Oil, Peanut Oil or Canola Oil
3	8	15	Carrots
2	4	8	Yellow or White Onions
3	8	15	Red Peppers
1	2	3	Kobucha Japanese Squash
2-6oz	4-6 oz	8-6 oz	Boneless/Skinless Chicken Breast (optional)
3	6	12	Diced Tomatoes
3 - 375ml cans	8 - 375 ml cans	15 - 375 ml cans	Coconut Milk
3 cups	8 cups	15 cups	Water
1 Tbsp	3 Tbsp	8 Tbsp	Chicken or Veggie Bouillon Base (or to taste)
2 Tbsp	5 Tbsp	7 Tbsp	Fish Sauce (or to taste)
1 Tsp	2 Tsp	1 Tbsp	Thai Chili Garlic Paste
1 ½ Tbsp	4 Tbsp	6 Tbsp	Green Curry Paste
5-6 coins	12-14 coins	18-20 coins	Ginger
1 Tbsp	3 Tbsp	5 Tbsp	Garlic
1 Tbsp	3 Tbsp	5 Tbsp	Cane Sugar
5	10	20	Kaffir Lime leaves
5-6 pieces	12-13 pieces	23-24 pieces	Lemon Grass
3	8	15	Limes (fresh squeezed juice only)
1 Tbsp	3 Tbsp	5 Tbsp	Basil or Cilantro leaves
225 g	300 g	454 g	Thai Rice Noodles (Optional)

Directions:

- Peel and dice carrots diagonally. Peel and dice squash and onions into medium-sized pieces. Wash and dice peppers and tomatoes into big chunks. Peel and mince garlic. Wash ginger and slice into thin coins.
- Cut the top off of the lemon grass and discard. Slice lemon grass in half, remove outside layer and cut lemon grass into 2 inch long pieces.
- In a large stock pot, heat oil and sauté diced chicken until cooked on the outside. Add garlic, ginger and onions and saute for a couple of minutes.
- Add fish sauce, green curry paste, chili paste and lemon grass and sauté until onions are soft.
- Skim the coconut milk off the top of the coconut water and add to above ingredients. Sauté until the oils from the curry paste start to show through. This helps enhance the curry flavors even more so.
- Add crushed kaffir lime leaves. Crush the kaffir lime leaves either by using your hands or in a mortar and pestle.
- Add cane sugar or palm sugar, the coconut water and stock.
- If adding Thai rice noodles, soak the noodles in either boiling water for a few minutes until soft or pour hot water over noodles and soak for 20 minutes or so until soft. Add to the soup right before serving so they don't become overcooked.
- Let the flavors merge and before serving add fresh squeezed lime juice and minced basil or cilantro.

Roasted Butternut Squash & Coconut Soup

A rich and warming soup made with deliciously seasoned roasted squash.

12 Servings	32 Servings	60 Servings	Ingredients
3 large	6 large	10 large	Butternut Squash
3-4 cloves	5-6 cloves	7-8 cloves	Garlic
1 Tbsp	3 Tbsp	5 Tbsp	Minced Ginger
2	3	4	Onions
3 - 398 ml cans	8 - 398 ml cans	15 - 398 ml cans	Coconut Milk
3 Tbsp	7 Tbsp	9 Tbsp	Maple Syrup or Brown Sugar
3 Tbsp	5 Tbsp	½ cup	Dry Chicken or Vegetable Bouillon Base (or to taste)
1 ½ cups	4 cups	7 cups	Water or Homemade Soup stock
1 ½ Tbsp	3 Tbsp	5 Tbsp	Curry Paste
1 Tbsp	2 Tbsp	4 Tbsp	Cumin
2 Tsp	1 Tbsp	2 Tbsp	Allspice
2	3	4	Bay Leaves
1 Tbsp	2 Tbsp	3 Tbsp	Sea Salt (or to taste)

Directions:

- Preheat oven to 375°F and tray out a large hotel sheet with parchment paper. Cut squash into cubes (leave skin on) and drizzle with maple syrup and sprinkle with cinnamon, cumin and allspice. Roast in oven for about 45 minutes or until the squash is tender.
- Peel and mince garlic and ginger.
- Peel and dice onions into small pieces.
- In a large stock pot, heat oil and sauté garlic, ginger and onions together until onions are soft.
- Add curry paste to taste. The amounts given in this recipe are a minimum as everyone has different heat tolerance. It is a lot easier to add more then to take away. If you find that you would like to add more, then add more! That

is the beauty of cooking…you are in control. Add cumin and allspice and sauté for a few more minutes.

- Add the roasted squash and sauté with the spices. Scoop the coconut milk off the top of the coconut water and add to the stock pot. Sauté until the oils from the curry begin to be released.
- Add coconut water, water and bouillon base to taste and, using a hand held blender, process soup together until well blended.
- Adjust seasonings and add salt, sweetener such as honey or agave syrup and bay leaves. Honey is best to use for curries as it helps enhance the flavors.
- Simmer until the flavors merge.

Minestrone

This hearty soup makes an excellent friend on a cold day.

12 Servings	32 Servings	60 Servings	Ingredients
2	3	4	Onion
3 cloves	6 cloves	12 cloves	Garlic
3 stalks	8 stalks	12 stalks	Celery
3	6	12	Carrots
1 ½ cups	3 cups	5 cups	Diced Zucchini
6 leaves	16 leaves	30 leaves	Kale or Chard (chopped)
1 ½ cups	3 cups	6 cups	Red Peppers
1 348 ml can	2 348 ml cans	3 348 ml cans	White Kidney Beans
1 ½ cups	3 cups	5 cups	Frozen Green Beans
6 TB (2 156 ml can)	9 Tbsp(3 156 ml c)	15 TB(4 cans)	Tomato Paste
1 - 540 ml cans	2 - 540 ml cans	3 - 540 ml cans	Diced Tomatoes + juice
12 cups	32 cups	60 cups	Water or Homemade soup stock
¼ cup	¾ cup	1 1/4 cups	Dry Chicken or Vegetarian Bouillon Base (or to taste)
1 Tbsp	3 Tbsp	5 Tbsp	Fresh Parsley
1 Tbsp	3 Tbsp	5 Tbsp	Basil
¾ cup	2 cups	4 cups	Elbow Macaroni
1 Tbsp	2 Tbsp	3 Tbsp	Sea Salt (or to taste)
½ Tbsp	1 Tbsp	2 Tbsp	Pepper (or to taste)
3 Tbsp	8 Tbsp	12 Tbsp	Dill
¾ cup	2 cups	4 cups	Parmesan

Directions:

- In a large pot, bring to a boil the salted water and add macaroni. Cook until al dente, about 8 minutes.
- Peel and dice onion into small pieces. Peel and mince garlic. Wash and dice zucchini, kale and pepper.
- In a large stock pot, over medium heat, heat oil and sauté onions and garlic for a few minutes. Add zucchini, peppers, carrots, and kale and sauté for a few minutes longer.
- Add water or home-made soup stock, chicken or vegetable stock to taste, basil and tomato paste and diced tomatoes.
- Add drained white kidney beans, frozen green beans, bay leaves and fresh minced parsley and dill.
- Add salt and pepper to taste and adjust seasonings. Add macaroni noodles just before serving.
- Sprinkle with parmesan.

Mexican Jumping Bean Soup

Ever seen a Mexican jumping bean? Me neither … but the flavors of this soup are sure to get you jumping.

12 Servings	32 Servings	60 Servings	Ingredients
3-4	8-10	15-17	Tomatoes
1	2	3	White Onions
2 stalks	8 stalks	15 stalks	Celery
3	7	15	Garlic Cloves
4 Tbsp	8 Tbsp	½ cup	Olive Oil
12 cups	32 cups	60 cups	Chicken or Vegetable Broth
1	3	5	Avocados
½ -348 ml can	1 -348 ml can	2 - 348 ml can	Black Beans
1 cup	3 cups	5 cups	Frozen corn
1 Tbsp	3 Tbsp	5 Tbsp	Minced Cilantro
1 Tsp	2 Tsp	3 Tsp	Dried Chipotle or Chilies
1 Tbsp	3 Tbsp	5 Tbsp	Ground Cumin
1 Tbsp	3 Tbsp	5 Tbsp	Chili powder
Tbsp	2 Tbsp	3 Tbsp	Sea Salt (or to taste)
1 Tsp	1 Tbsp	2 Tbsp	Pepper (or to taste)
1 cup	8 cups	15 cups	Sour Cream
6 cups	16 cups	30 cups	Tortilla Chips

Directions:

- Place whole tomatoes in a large pot of cold water, bring to a boil and boil for a couple of minutes. Remove tomatoes from water and, once cooled, place them in a food processor. Wash and chop celery to medium-sized pieces and place in food processor. Peel garlic and onions and place in food processor with tomatoes and blend together.
- In a medium sauce pan, heat oil over medium heat and add tomato purée and heat slowly until the tomatoes change a nice deep red color and have a pleasant taste.

- In a medium pan over medium heat, roast minced chilies, dried cumin and chili powder for a few minutes until the flavors have been released.
- Add roasted chilies, cumin and chili powder to the tomato and onion purée.
- Add chicken or veggie broth and simmer until the flavors merge. Add salt and pepper to taste.
- Meanwhile, peel and dice avocado. Cut tortillas in half and then cut crosswise into ½ inch strips and set aside in a bowl.
- Add diced avocado prior to serving. Serve with a handful of tortillas on top and a dollop of sour cream.

French Onion Soup

A heart-warming soup full of flavor and can be made vegetarian.

12 Servings	32 Servings	60 Servings	Ingredients
3	8	15	Yellow Onions
3	5	8	Garlic cloves
3 Tbsp	5 Tbsp	8 Tbsp	Butter
3 Tbsp	5 Tbsp	8 Tbsp	Olive Oil
1 Tbsp	3 Tbsp	5 Tbsp	Dried Thyme
12 cups	32 cups	60 cups	Vegetarian or Beef Broth
1 cup	3 cups	5 cups	Tamari or Soya Sauce
¾ cup	1 ½ cups	1 ½ cups	Red Wine or Red Wine Vinegar or Sherry
2	4	6	Bay Leaves
1 Tsp	1 Tbsp	2 Tbsp	Sea Salt (or to taste)
½ Tsp	½ Tbsp	1 Tbsp	Pepper (or to taste)
3 cups	8 cups	15 cups	Swiss or gruyere cheese
6 cups	16 cups	30 cups	Crusty Italian Loaf or leftover croutons

Directions:

- Peel and cut onion in half and slice into half-moon strips.
- In a medium large stock pot, heat butter and olive oil over medium low heat.
- Add onions and sauté for about ½ hour to 45 minutes until onions are caramelized. Add thyme to onions once they begin to soften. Peel and mince garlic with a garlic press, add to sautéing onions and cook for about 5 minutes.
- Once onions have become caramelized, deglaze the pan with red wine, red wine vinegar or sherry and reduce until the liquids have reduced to half the amount.
- Add broth, tamari, soya sauce, bay leaves and salt and pepper to taste.

- Simmer lightly until the flavors merge.
- Serve with toasted ciabatta croutons or another type of cubed crusty bread placed on top and a handful of shredded Swiss or gruyère cheese or other sharp cheese.

SENSATIONAL SIDE DISHES

Ratatouille

This bright and colorful dish makes an excellent side dish with a robust, full flavor.

12 Servings	32 Servings	60 Servings	Ingredients
3 Tbsp	5 Tbsp	8 Tbsp	Olive Oil
3 Tbsp	5 Tbsp	8 Tbsp	Crushed Garlic
3	7	10	Onions
3	8	15	Green and Red Peppers (Sweet Bell)
1 head	2 heads	3 heads	Cauliflower
3 - 540 ml can	1 - 2.4L can	2 - 2.4 L cans	Tomatoes with juice
5 stalks	1 bunch	2 bunches	Celery
2	5	8	Zucchini
½ kg	2 kg	4 kg	Mushrooms
1	1 ½	2	Eggplant
1 Tbsp	3 Tbsp	5 Tbsp	Cumin
¼ cup	½ cup	¾ cup	Balsamic Vinegar
3 Tbsp	8 Tbsp	15 Tbsp	Basil
3 Tbsp	8 Tbsp	15 Tbsp	Oregano
3 Tbsp	8 Tbsp	15 Tbsp	Parsley
3 Tbsp	8 Tbsp	12 Tbsp	Thyme (fresh or dried)
1 Tbsp	3 Tbsp	5 Tbsp	Garlic Powder
2	4	6	Bay Leaves
1 Tbsp	2 Tbsp	3 Tbsp	Salt
1 Tbsp	2 Tbsp	3 Tbsp	Pepper

Directions:

- Wash zucchini, eggplant, peppers and celery. Remove membrane from peppers. Dice zucchini, peppers and eggplant into large pieces.
- Cut celery into medium-sized pieces. You want all the veggies to be cut or cubed into large pieces so they hold together during the slow roasting period. Pieces should be about ½ inch in size.
- Peel and dice onion into medium-sized pieces.

- Wash and half mushrooms. Cut cauliflower head in half and remove the bottom. Break into bite-sized pieces and wash prior to use.
- Peel and mince garlic. Toss diced veggies and garlic in olive oil.
- Pre heat oven to 325°F and in a large roasting pan combine veggies, garlic, diced canned tomatoes including juice, all the spices (cumin, oregano, thyme, basil, garlic powder, salt/pepper) and bay leaves. Add balsamic vinegar and mix together.
- Leave uncovered and cook slowly until almost tender, stirring occasionally. Veggies have a tendency to shrink considerably the longer you cook them, so it is important to cook only 1 ½ hours before serving and serve right away.

Red Lentil Curry

A rich and hearty lentil curry that can be served as a side or a main. As with any curry dish, I always recommend adding ingredients such as curry pastes, curry powders and cayenne pepper to taste. It is easier to add ingredients than to take away.

12 Servings	32 Servings	60 Servings	Ingredients
4 cups	12 cups	22 cups	Red Lentils
2	5	8	Onions
3 Tbsp	8 Tbsp	12 Tbsp	Vegetable Oil or Clarified Ghee
2Tbsp	4 Tbsp	7 Tbsp	Mild Curry Paste (or to taste)
1 1/2 Tbsp	3 Tbsp	5 Tbsp	Mild Curry Powder
1 Tbsp	3 Tbsp	5 Tbsp	Ground Turmeric
1 Tbsp	3 Tbsp	5 Tbsp	Ground Cumin
1 Tbsp	3 Tbsp	5 Tbsp	Ground Coriander
1 Tsp	½ Tbsp	1 Tbsp	Cayenne Pepper (or to taste)
1 Tbsp	2 Tbsp	3 Tbsp	Himalayan or Sea Salt (or to taste)
¼ cup	½ cup	1 cup	Honey (or to taste)
3 Tbsp	5 Tbsp	8 Tbsp	Minced Garlic
3 Tbsp	5 Tbsp	8 Tbsp	Minced Ginger
1 - 178 ml can	2 - 178 ml cans	3 - 178 ml cans	Tomato Purée

Directions:

- Wash the lentils in cold water and rinse until water runs clear. This step is very important as it helps reduce any "scumminess" that might accumulate when boiling the lentils. Place the lentils in a medium to medium large pot and cover with water and simmer until lentils are just about tender, approximately 40 minutes. Be sure not to overcook. Once lentils are cooked, drain them but reserve about 1/3 of the water and set aside until ready to use.
- Peel and finely dice the onions and sauté them, using a medium-sized stock pot, in clarified ghee or oil until they become translucent. While the onions are cooking, peel and mince garlic and ginger and combine with the curry paste, curry powder, turmeric, cumin, cayenne, coriander and salt in a mixing bowl.

- Add curry mixture to the onions and cook over medium heat for a couple of minutes longer until the flavors are released, stirring often to prevent spices from burning.
- Add tomato paste and honey. Mix well before adding the lentils. Add the lentils, stirring often, and simmer gently until the flavors merge.
- Serve with naan bread and brown basmati rice.

Moussaka with Greek Béchamel

A savory side and really easy to make!

12 Servings	32 Servings	60 Servings	Ingredients
3	8	15	Eggplant
1 Tbsp	3 Tbsp	5 Tbsp	Salt
2 cups	5 cups	8 cups	Flour
8-9	20-24	36-40	Red Potatoes
6 cups	16 cups	30 cups	Vegetarian Tomato Sauce
1 Tbsp	2 Tbsp	4 Tbsp	Cinnamon
3 cup	8 cups	15 cups	Plain Yogurt, preferably Greek
1 Tbsp	3 Tbsp	5 Tbsp	Lemon Juice
5	10	15	Eggs
½ Tbsp	1 ½ Tbsp	3 Tbsp	Nutmeg
3 cups	8 cups	15 cups	Parmesan
3 cups	8 cups	15 cups	Mozzarella
6 Tbsp	9 Tbsp	15 Tbsp	Olive Oil/Butter
2 Tbsp	5 Tbsp	8 Tbsp	Parsley

Directions:

- Slice eggplant lengthwise and place a single layer of eggplant on a cookie sheet over some paper towel.
- Sprinkle with half of the salt and let stand for 20 minutes. The salt will draw out any bitterness. Repeat layers until you have used up the eggplant. Once the eggplant has started to sweat, blot with paper towel.
- Thinly slice potatoes and add to cold water. Add the remainder of the salt to potatoes. Boil until just tender and remove from heat, drain and let cool.
- Heat frying pan with either butter or oil. Dredge eggplant in flour. Lightly fry each side until golden brown. Set eggplant aside.
- Refer to Basic Meat Sauce Recipe. Heat sauce in a large stock pot and add cinnamon to the sauce.

- Mix yogurt, eggs, lemon juice and parmesan together. Add nutmeg, salt and pepper.
- Grate mozzarella and set aside.
- Using a 2 inch deep hotel pan, coat with Pam and layer casserole, starting with the eggplant first. Add a layer of potatoes, then top with a layer of tomato sauce. Add the traditional Greek béchamel sauce. Repeat layering two more times. Finish with a nice thick layer of mozzarella and sprinkle with parsley.
- Preheat oven to 375°F and cover with hotel lid or plastic wrap and tinfoil placed over top (to prevent plastic from melting) and bake until sauce is bubbling around the edges, about 45 minutes. Remove lid and bake until slightly browned on top. Let stand for 10 minutes, then slice into squares before serving.
- Serve with Couscous.

Fettuccini Alfredo

If you are looking for a healthier option for thickening, I suggest using spelt flour. It is a surprisingly versatile flour that I use for thickening white sauces or gravy.

12 Servings	32 Servings	60 Servings	Ingredients
1 cup	2 cups	3 cups	Butter
1	2	3	Onions
1/2 cup	3/4 cup	1 1/4 cup	White Flour or Spelt Flour
3 (or 2 Tbsp)	8 (or 5 Tbsp)	15 (or 8 Tbsp)	Garlic Cloves
4 ½ cups	12 cups	22 1/2 cups	Heavy Whipping Cream
1Tbsp	2 Tbsp	3 Tbsp	Nutmeg
1 Tbsp	4 Tbsp	7 Tbsp	Vegetable/Chicken Stock
2	4	5	Bay Leaves
¾ Tsp	2 Tbsp	3 Tbsp	Cracked Pepper (or to taste)
½ Tbsp	1 Tbsp	2 Tbsp	Sea Salt (or to taste)
3 cups	8 cups	15 cups	Grated Parmesan

Directions:

- In a medium-sized stock pot, melt butter over low heat. Peel onions, slice in half and dice into small pieces. Sauté onions until they become translucent in color. Using a garlic press, peel and mince garlic. Add minced garlic to the onions and sauté for a couple of minutes. Add flour and mix well with butter until a smooth paste forms.
- Add only a bit of cream, nutmeg, dry stock, cracked pepper and parmesan. Stir constantly until parmesan has begun to melt.
- Add the remainder of the whipping cream and bay leaves and bring to a light simmer until all the parmesan has been melted. Do not boil cream sauces or they will curdle.
- Serve over fettuccini noodles. Note: Do not rinse the noodles after boiling as the gluten from the water helps to thicken the sauce.
- For something different try adding frozen peas, tarragon, pesto or roasted, sliced chicken as a main.

Grilled Balsamic Broccoli

A splash of flavor on plain old broccoli.

12 Servings	32 Servings	60 Servings	Ingredients
6 heads	15 heads	30 heads	Broccoli
¼ cup	¾ cup	1 ¼ cup	Balsamic vinegar
6 Tbsp	¾ cup	1 ¼ cup	Olive Oil
¾ tsp	1 Tbsp	3 Tbsp	Cracked Pepper (or to taste)
¾ tsp	2 tsp	3 ¾ tsp	Sea Salt (or to taste)
1 Tbsp	2 ½ Tbsp	4 Tbsp	Mrs. Dash Seasoning

Directions:

- Wash and cut broccoli lengthwise into long pieces and toss in oil, sea salt, pepper, balsamic and Mrs. Dash seasoning.
- Heat BBQ or grill to medium low, grill the broccoli on medium heat until lightly browned. Serve immediately.
- ***Quick Tip:*** When cooking vegetables on a grill, add a splash of water to help the veggies cook faster. Be careful not burn yourself from the steam!

Rice

Rice cooked in the oven turns out every time and is extremely easy to prepare. I use a large hotel insert when cooking for larger quantities. If cooking rice in a hotel pan, you can add the correct measurements or use this little trick: add the water until it is just at the middle knuckle of your middle finger. Typically, I average about ¼ cup of dry rice per person, but I always make a little extra to use in soups.

Below is a list of the different varieties of rice most commonly used:

- ***Jasmine:*** Fragrant rice from Thailand typically used in Thai dishes.
- ***Basmati:*** Sold in both white and brown varieties and is used in making Indian dishes.
- ***Parboiled:*** Partially cooked rice which still has the husk on it, making it almost as nutritionally sound as brown rice and takes half the time to cook. For every cup of rice, add 1 ½ cups of water.
- ***Brown:*** Nutritionally dense, nutty tasting grain available in different varieties. Takes twice as long as parboiled rice and for every cup of water add 2 cups of water. Tip: If you find that you have overcooked the brown rice and it has turned out sticky, turn it into a risotto by adding grated parmesan, ground cracked pepper, sundried tomatoes and frozen peas and mixing well until the cheese has melted and peas have thawed out from the hot rice.
- ***Arborio Rice:*** Also known as risotto or Italian rice, this is a short grain rice that can absorb a lot of liquid before becoming fully cooked.

12 Servings	32 Servings	60 Servings	Ingredients
6 cups	15 cups	28 cups	Parboiled Rice
9 cups	22 ½ cups	42 cups	Water
2 Tbsp	4 Tbsp	8 Tbsp	Dry Chicken or Vegetable Stock
2 Tbsp	4 Tbsp	8 Tbsp	Butter

Directions:

- Preheat oven to 350°F.
- Rinse rice before cooking under cold water until the water runs clear.
- Pour rice into a large hotel pan. When cooking larger amounts of rice, over 32 servings, I recommend separating the rice into two hotel pans as rice doubles in volume when cooked.

- Add butter and stock and give a little stir.
- Cover with plastic wrap and tinfoil. I prefer using this method rather than a hotel lid as it keeps the moisture in and you don't end up with dried out rice. Use a commercial plastic wrap and tinfoil that can withstand the heat from the oven. Plastic wrap covered with tinfoil will not melt into the food. Take caution to not scald yourself from the escaping steam when removing the tinfoil and plastic wrap.
- Cook for 1 ½ - 2 hours depending on the stove. Remove from oven, let cool slightly and fluff with a fork.

Lemon Rice

A zesty rice that goes well with any Greek meal.

12 Servings	32 Servings	60 Servings	Ingredients
6 cups	15 cups	28 cups	Parboiled Rice
3 cups	9 cups	18 cups	Lemon Juice from concentrate
6 cups	13 cups	26 cups	Water
1 Tbsp	2 Tbsp	4 Tbsp	Dry Chicken or Vegetable Stock
3 tsp	5 tsp	8 tsp	Parsley
2 Tbsp	4 Tbsp	8 Tbsp	Butter
1 Tbsp	3 Tbsp	5 Tbsp	Minced Garlic

Directions:

- Preheat oven to 350°F.
- Rinse water under cold water until the water runs clear.
- Let rice sit in lemon juice for an hour or so to soak up some of the lemon flavor. Add minced garlic, parsley (fresh parsley or dried will work), butter and stock and give a little stir.
- Add water to rice and cover with plastic wrap and tinfoil.
- Cook for 1 ½ half - 2 hours depending on the oven. Remove from oven, let cool slightly and fluff with a fork.

Rice Pulao

A fragrant blend of Indian spices and is a must for any Indian meal. For a heallthier option substitute brown basmati for white.

12 Servings	32 Servings	60 Servings	Ingredients
6 cups	15 cups	28 cups	White Basmati Rice
9 cups	22 ½ cups	42 cups	Water
1 cup	3 cups	5 cups	Frozen Peas & Carrots
1 ½ Tbsp	3 Tbsp	5 Tbsp	Clarified Butter
1 Tbsp	2 Tbsp	3 Tbsp	Cardamom Pods
3-4	8-9	12-15	Cloves
1 Tbsp	3 Tbsp	7 Tbsp	Turmeric
1 ½ Tbsp	3 Tbsp	5 Tbsp	Dry Chicken or Vegetable Stock

Directions:

- Preheat oven to 350°F.
- Prior to cooking, rinse basmati rice under cold water until water is clear.
- In a large hotel pan, add rice, stock, butter, spices and frozen veggies.
- Cover with plastic wrap and tinfoil.
- If cooking brown basmati add ½ cup of water to 1 ½ cups of water in the above measurements and cook for approximately 2 hours or until soft and fluffs with a fork. Reduce cooking time for white basmati by ½ hour. Remove cover and fluff with a fork.
- Quick tip: If you are in a pinch and need the rice done in a hurry, add boiling water the rice and cook at 400°F for an hour or until done.
- Serve with butter chicken, curried veggies, naan bread and mango chutney.

Mexican Rice

A flavorful alternative to plain old rice… I use packaged taco seasoning which helps to save time when cooking for large quantities but look for a low sodium variety.

12 Servings	32 Servings	60 Servings	Ingredients
5 cups	15 cups	28 cups	Parboiled Rice
8 cups	22 ½ cups	42 cups	Water
1 - 250 ml can	2 - 250 ml cans	3 - 250 ml cans	Tomato Paste
1 - 540 ml can	4 - 540 ml cans	1 - 2.4 L can	Diced Tomatoes
1 - 250 ml can	2 - 250 ml cans	3 - 250 ml cans	Black Beans (rinsed and drained)
80 g	120 g	160 g	Taco Seasoning
2	3	4	Onions
1 ½ Tbsp	3 Tbsp	5 Tbsp	Chicken Stock
2 Tbsp	4 Tbsp	8 Tbsp	Butter or non-hydrogenated Margarine

Directions:

- Preheat oven to 350°F.
- Rinse rice under cold water until water runs clear. This will remove any by-products that have may have found their way in.
- In a large hotel pan, combine rice and water.
- Peel and dice onions and add to rice and water.
- Stir in diced tomatoes and juice, tomato paste, black beans, taco seasoning, chicken stock and butter.
- Cover with plastic wrap and tinfoil and cook for an hour and a half. Carefully remove cover and fluff with a fork.

Greek Roasted Potatoes

Marinate these potatoes for a couple hours so they can absorb some of the lemon flavor – Yum!

12 Servings	32 Servings	60 Servings	Ingredients
20 large	60 large	120 large	Red Potatoes
6 Tbsp	12 Tbsp	20 Tbsp	Minced Garlic
2 Tbsp	6 Tbsp	12 Tbsp	Oregano
1 ½ cups	4 cups	7 cups	Lemon Juice
3 tsp	8 tsp	15 tsp	Paprika
2 Tbsp	4 Tbsp	8 Tbsp	Salt (or to taste)
6 Tbsp	8 Tbsp	15 Tbsp	Oil

Directions:

- Preheat oven to 350°F.
- Cut potatoes into wedges. Quick Tip: Keep wedges in cold water until finished cutting all the potatoes so the potatoes don't turn grey.
- Lightly boil potatoes so that they are semi-soft, not cooked but soft enough that they will be able to absorb some of the lemon flavor.
- In a large bowl, combine garlic, lemon juice, paprika, salt, oregano and oil.
- Drain water from potatoes and soak in the garlic and lemon juice mixture for about an hour.
- On a large hotel sheet, place parchment on bottom and tray out potatoes onto sheet. Cook at 400°F for 45 minutes to an hour, turning at least once.

Rosemary Roasted Potatoes

Fresh rosemary is key for this scrumptious recipe.

12 Servings	32 Servings	60 Servings	Ingredients
20 large	60 large	120 large	Red Potatoes
6 Tbsp	8 Tbsp	15 Tbsp	Minced Garlic
4 Tbsp	10 Tbsp	1 cup	Chopped Fresh Rosemary
3 tsp	8 tsp	15 tsp	Paprika
2 Tbsp	4 Tbsp	8 Tbsp	Salt (or to taste)
6 Tbsp	8 Tbsp	15 Tbsp	Oil

Directions:

- Preheat oven to 400°F.
- Wash and cut potatoes into ¼ inch wedges.
- Quick Tip: Keep in cold water until finished cutting all the potatoes so that the potatoes don't turn grey.
- Drain water from potatoes and pat dry. The water left on the potatoes will actually cause them to boil in the oven rather than roast.
- Peel and mince the garlic. Finely mince the fresh rosemary.
- Mix garlic, minced rosemary, paprika, salt and oil and coat potatoes. On a large hotel sheet lay potatoes on sheet, making sure to not overlap and cook at 400°F for an hour to an hour and half, depending on the oven, turning at least once until golden brown.

Variation: Add chopped fresh dill instead of rosemary or try garlic and herb cream cheese spread over the potatoes.

Roasted Vegetables with Fennel & Turmeric

A colorful explosion of root vegetables with a subtle hint of fennel and the surprisingly nutty taste of roasted kale.

12 Servings	32 Servings	60 Servings	Ingredients
3	8	15	Onions
3	8	15	Carrots
6 stalks	2 bunches	4 bunches	Celery
3 cups	8 cups	15 cups	Butternut/Acorn Squash
6	8	15	Parsnips
6	8	15	Beets
2 each	4 each	8 each	Red/Yellow/Orange Peppers
1 bunch	3 bunches	5 bunches	Kale
1 whole bulb	2 whole bulbs	3 whole bulbs	Garlic
2 bulbs	4 bulbs	6 bulbs	Fennel
1 tsp	2 Tbsp	4 Tbsp	Turmeric
1 Tbsp	3 Tbsp	5 Tbsp	Olive Oil
1 Tbsp	3 Tbsp	5 Tbsp	Course Salt

Directions:

- Preheat oven to 375°F.
- Peel veggies and dice onions, carrots, celery, squash and parsnips into cubes. Peel garlic and add cloves to veggies.
- Cut top off fennel bulb and place anise herb aside. Peel the outer layer of the fennel bulb and slice bulb lengthwise into long strips.
- Remove anise from stalk and mince finely. If you can't find fresh anise then simply omit and use fresh rosemary instead.
- In a large bowl or roasting pan place veggies together, except the kale, and cover veggies with olive oil, turmeric, salt and anise. Set kale aside and lightly toss in olive oil and salt and add to the other vegetables 20 minutes before they are finished. Kale takes no time to bake and will get overcooked.

- Using a large hotel sheet pan, place parchment on hotel sheet and spread evenly with veggies. Bake until veggies fall off fork, approximately 1 - 1 ½ hours, turning them every so often. Be sure not overcook as roasted veggies shrink considerably the longer you cook them.

Sautéed Bok Choy with Pineapple & Oyster Sauce

Delicious either served as a side with Thai Green curry or as a main dish over rice.

12 Servings	32 Servings	60 Servings	Ingredients
12 heads	32 heads	60 heads	Baby Bok Choy
2 – 348 ml can	1 - 1L can	1 - 2.4 L	Canned Pineapple + juice
4 Tbsp	¼ cup	½ cup	Peanut Oil or Vegetable Oil
2 cups	5 cups	1 - 1L can	Oyster Sauce
6 cloves	8 cloves	15 cloves	Minced Garlic
3 Tbsp	8 Tbsp	1 cup	Sweet Chili Sauce

Directions:

- Wash and slice bok choy on an angle into chunky pieces. The bok choy will shrink considerably, so you want it to hold up during the sautéing process by cutting it into larger pieces.
- Heat oil in a large wok or on a flat top grill, add the bok choy and garlic and sauté for a few minutes. Add pineapple and juice, oyster sauce and sweet chili sauce to mixture and sauté gently for a couple of minutes.
- Serve with Fried Rice or with Thai dishes. Must be served right away.

Simple Swiss Chard

If you wish to extend this dish, simply add some julienned peppers.

12 Servings	32 Servings	60 Servings	Ingredients
6 bunches	15 bunches	30 bunches	Swiss Chard
6 cloves	12 cloves	20 cloves	Minced Garlic
2 Tbsp	5 Tbsp	8 Tbsp	Olive Oil
3 Tbsp	8 Tbsp	12 Tbsp	Balsamic Oil
1 Tbsp	2 Tbsp	3 Tbsp	Agave Syrup
1 Tbsp	2 Tbsp	3 Tbsp	Sesame Seeds

Directions:

- Wash and chop swiss chard into small pieces.
- Peel and mince garlic.
- Heat oil on a flat grill or in a large commercial frying pan.
- Mix together garlic, vinegar and agave syrup and pour over Swiss chard.
- Sauté swiss chard on medium heat for a few minutes until soft.

Roasted Vegetable Strudel with Balsamic Reduction

Serve this simple yet irresistible dish to vegetarians and guarantee they will love every bite!

12 Servings	32 Servings	60 Servings	Ingredients
2 cups	5 cups	10 cups	Squash
2	5	10	Zucchini
2	5	10	Red Peppers
3 cups	8 cups	18 cups	Brown Mushrooms
6 cloves	9 cloves	15 cloves	Minced Garlic
1 ½ cups	4 cups	7 cups	Ricotta
1 Tbsp	2 Tbsp	3 Tbsp	Sea Salt (or to taste)
1 Tbsp	2 Tbsp	3 Tbsp	Cracked Pepper (or to taste)
1 cup	1 ½ cups	2 cups	Whole Wheat Bread Crumbs
1 ½ Tbsp	2 Tbsp	3 Tbsp	Oregano
3 Tbsp	8 Tbsp	12 Tbsp	Thyme
2 tsp	1 Tbsp	2 Tbsp	Crushed Fennel Seeds
¾ cup	1 ¼ cup	2 cups	Goat Cheese or Feta
1 454 g pkg	2 454 g pkg	3 454 g packages	Phyllo

Directions:

- Preheat oven to 350°F.
- Wash and dice squash, zucchini and red peppers into medium-sized chunks.
- Wash and dry mushrooms and peel garlic.
- In a medium-sized pan combine zucchini, red peppers, mushrooms and whole garlic cloves. Drizzle with olive oil and add salt and pepper. Do the same with the squash, but place it in a separate roasting dish as it will take longer to roast.
- Roast veggies for about 35 minutes or until lightly browned on the outside.
- Meanwhile, combine breadcrumbs, ricotta, goat cheese or feta, oregano, crushed fennel (crush using a mortar and pestle) and thyme.

- Once roasted veggies are done, add to above mixture and purée in a food processor. You want it to be a bit chunky and not too mushy. I suggest purée-ing the mixture for a couple of minutes, stopping every few seconds.
- Melt butter over medium heat. Set aside.
- Lay thawed phyllo sheets on a damp towel. Using two sheets at a time, lay them flat on a working area and place a couple of tablespoons of puréed mixture near the edge closest to you. Make sure to place another damp towel over the phyllo to prevent them from drying out.
- Fold the mixture over once, then place a dab of butter on each end of the phyllo sheets and fold over the right and left sides into the middle.
- Next dab the top of the phyllo with butter and fold away from you again until you have a nice rectangular package.
- Place seam side down and dot with butter on the top of the phyllo.
- Bake at 375°F for 35 - 40 minutes until browned on top. Serve with balsamic reduction lightly drizzled across each strudel.

Balsamic Reduction

Adds a nice touch to a multitude of dishes – try experimenting. You might want to open a window when preparing this recipe as the vinegar becomes quite strong as it simmers.

12 Servings	32 Servings	60 Servings	Ingredients
1 1/2 cups	4 cups	7 cups	Balsamic Vinegar
1 Tbsp	3 Tbsp	5 Tbsp	Honey, Agave Syrup or Cane Sugar

Directions:

- In a medium-sized pot, bring balsamic vinegar to a boil and then turn down to a mere simmer.
- Add sweetener and let simmer until the reduction thickens into syrup.
- ***Quick Tip:*** Let cool slightly, pour into a squeeze bottle and use when needed. Place squeeze bottle into warm water to make the syrup squeezable.

Portobello Mushroom Stack with Goat Cheese & Balsamic Reduction

A hearty vegetarian dish with the sophisticated flavors of goat cheese, sundried tomatoes and balsamic.

12 Servings	32 Servings	60 Servings	Ingredients
18	45	90	Portobello Mushrooms
9 cups	22 cups	45 cups	Fresh Spinach
3 cups	8 cups	15 cups	Sundried Tomatoes
1 ½ cups	4 cups	7 cups	Herbed Chèvre
1 Tbsp	2 Tbsp	3 Tbsp	Sea Salt
1 Tbsp	2 Tbsp	3 Tbsp	Cracked Pepper
¾ cup	2 cups	4 cups	Pine Nuts
½ cup	1 cup	1 ½ cups	Balsamic Reduction

Directions:

- In a medium-sized stock pot, bring water to a boil. Place spinach in the pot and boil until the spinach has shrunk considerably and is tender. Strain, let cool and wring out any excess water with your hands and set spinach aside.
- Wash Portobello mushrooms really well and pat dry. Using olive oil, oil both sides and sprinkle salt and pepper on both sides as well. Line mushrooms on a large cookie sheet. Preheat oven to 350°F and bake the mushrooms for about 30 minutes. Flip half way through and bake on both sides.
- Meanwhile, chop sundried tomatoes and combine with goat chèvre.
- Mix spinach with cracked pepper and sea salt to taste.
- Using a cookie sheet spread out pine nuts and roast in the oven for 30 – 40 minutes.
- Remove mushrooms from the oven and top with spinach, chèvre, pine nuts and drizzle with balsamic reduction.
- Place in oven and reduce oven temperature to 300°F. Bake for another 10 minutes.

Fettuccini with Roasted Garlic & Sundried Tomatoes

Such a satisfying dish and full of flavour so no one will ever know how easy it is to make!

12 Servings	32 Servings	60 Servings	Ingredients
6 cups	16 cups	30 cups	Fettuccini Noodles
12 cups	24 cups	45 cups	Water
1 Tbsp	2 Tbsp	3 Tbsp	Salt for water
3 bulbs	8 bulbs	15 bulbs	Roasted Garlic
1 Tbsp	1 ½ Tbsp	2 Tbsp	Cracked Pepper
6 cups	16 cups	30 cups	Sundried Tomatoes packed in oil
2 cups	5 cups	8 cups	Olive Oil
2 cups	3 cups	6 cups	Fresh Parmesan Cheese
1 tsp	½ Tbsp	1 Tbsp	Sea Salt (or to taste)

Directions:

- Coat garlic bulbs in olive oil and roast in oven at 350°F for 45 minutes.
- Once cooled, peel garlic and place into food processor. Add sundried tomatoes and oil from sundried tomato jar, salt and pepper to taste and olive oil. Pulse until completely mixed.
- In a large pot, bring water to a boil and place Fettuccini noodles in boiling water until noodle edges turn white. Mix together sauce, cracked pepper and noodles and serve.
- Sprinkle with fresh parmesan cheese. Adjust salt and pepper seasoning to taste.

Greek Pasta Toss

This dish came to me during a dinner service when I realized I was running low on Greek potatoes so in went the pasta and out came this creation!

12 Servings	32 Servings	60 Servings	Ingredients
6 cups	16 cups	30 cups	Fusili Noodles
12 cups	24 cups	45 cups	Water
1 Tbsp	2 Tbsp	3 Tbsp	Salt for water
¾ cups	2 cups	3 ¾ cups	Olive Oil
5 cups	18 cups	32 cups	Fresh Spinach
¾ cups	2 cups	4 cups	Sliced Black Olives
1 ½ cups	4 cups	7 ½ cups	Feta
2 Tbsp	4 Tbsp	7 Tbsp	Lemon Juice (or to taste)
3 Tbsp	8 Tbsp	15 Tbsp	Oregano
1 ½ Tbsp	4 Tbsp	8 Tbsp	Basil
3 Tbsp	8 Tbsp	15 Tbsp	Minced Garlic
6 Tbsp	1 cup	2 cups	Pine Nuts
1 1/2 Tbsp	3 Tbsp	5 Tbsp	Sea Salt (or to taste)
1 1/2 Tbsp	3 Tbsp	5 Tbsp	Cracked Pepper (or to taste)

Directions:

- In a large stockpot, boil salted water and add fusili noodles to boiling water.
- Stir every few minutes to prevent the noodles from sticking to the bottom of the pot and cook until slightly tender, about 20 minutes. The outside edges of the noodles should have turned white.
- Drain noodles and add spinach to hot noodles. Adding the spinach to the hot noodles will cook the spinach and it will shrink considerably.
- In a bowl, mix olive oil, olives, feta, lemon juice, minced garlic, oregano, basil, sea salt, cracked pepper and pine nuts.
- Mix the olive oil mixture with the pasta and spinach. Adjust the seasoning if needed and serve right away.

Option: Add marinated souvlaki chicken and serve as a main.

Pad Thai

As with most Thai dishes, this dish should encompass the flavors of salty (fish sauce), sweet (cane sugar), sour (tamarind) and spicy (chilies). Pad Thai is not as spicy as other traditional Thai dishes.

12 Servings	32 Servings	60 Servings	Ingredients
2 454 g packages	8 454 g pkgs	12 454 g pkgs	Medium Broad Rice Noodles
5	16	30	Eggs
6 Tbsp	8 Tbsp	12 Tbsp	Vegetable or Coconut Oil
7-9 cloves	18-20 cloves	30-34 cloves	Garlic
1 350 g Block	2 350 g Blocks	4 350 g Blocks	Extra Firm Tofu
3	8	15	Carrots
1 ½ cups	4 cups	7 cups	Bean Sprouts
6 Tbsp	1 cup	2 cups	Green Onions or Chives
6 Tbsp	1 cup	2 cups	Dry Roasted Peanuts
1 Tsp	1 Tbsp	2 Tbsp	Dried Chillies
1 Tbsp	3 Tbsp	5 Tbsp	Fish Sauce
1 ½ cups	4 ½ cups	10 cups(2.4 L)	Oyster Sauce
¾ cup	1 ½ cups	3 cups	Tamarind Paste or Concentrate
1/3 cup	½ cup	1 cup	Hot Water
½ cup	1 cup	2 cups	Sweet Thai Chilli Sauce
3 Tbsp	½ cup	1 cup	Cane Sugar or Brown Sugar
1 Tbsp	3 Tbsp	5 Tbsp	Apple Cider Vinegar/ White vinegar/or non-seasoned Rice Vinegar
3	8	15	Limes

Directions:

- Boil hot water and in a large stock pot, soak the rice noodles until just about soft (about 30 minutes) and drain.
- Peel and chop garlic into small pieces. Strain and dice tofu into small cubes. Peel and julienne the carrots into semi-long thin pieces. Set the ingredients aside.
- Mix together the fish sauce, oyster sauce, sweet Thai hot sauce, sugar, vinegar, tamarind paste and hot water. If using tamarind concentrate, you may find that you need more hot water added to the mixture.
- Crack eggs into a large bowl, mix with a fork and set aside.
- Using a pestle and mortar crush peanuts into small bits. If you don't have a pestle and mortar a knife will work just fine.
- Finely chop green onions or chives.
- Heat oil either in a large wok or on a flat top grill and lightly sauté tofu until golden brown. I find coconut oil gives this dish the most flavors. Add the carrot sticks, garlic and chillies and sauté for a few minutes. Remove from hot grill once tofu is browned.
- Mix the noodles and sauce together with a spatula or a wooden spoon to help gently separate the noodles and allow the sauce to coat all the noodles. Once the sauce and the noodles have been incorporated, add to grill and mix in the tofu, garlic, carrots and chilies.
- Push the noodles aside and add the eggs in batches, cooking for a couple of minutes and then folding the eggs into the noodles until the egg is cooked.
- Add finely chopped green onions or chives and bean sprouts and toss until soft. Garnish with peanuts and squeezed lime.

BBQ Veggie Skewers

A colourful array of veggies. I recommend boiling the mushrooms before placing them on the skewer; they are more appetizing this way.

12 Servings	32 Servings	60 Servings	Ingredients
18	48	90	Cherry Tomatoes
18	48	90	Mushrooms
3	8	15	Yellow or White Onions
3	8	15	Green Peppers
1	4	7	Zucchini
4 Tbsp	8 Tbsp	1 Cup	Olive Oil
1/2 Tbsp	1 Tbsp	2 Tbsp	Sea Salt
1/2 Tbsp	1 Tbsp	2 Tbsp	Pepper
24	64	120	Skewers

Directions:

- Soak skewers in water to prevent them burning on the barbeque.
- Wash the veggies except the onion and set aside.
- Fill a large pot with water and bring to a boil. Add the mushrooms and boil slightly until just about tender. This step is not absolutely necessary, but it will make the mushrooms taste and cook better.
- Slice peppers in half and remove membranes. Dice peppers into large ¼ inch pieces..
- Slice zucchini in half and cut into half-moon pieces that are ½ inch thick.
- Peel and cut onion in half and dice into ½ inch pieces.
- Toss peppers, zucchini, mushrooms, cherry tomatoes and onion in olive oil and salt and pepper to taste.
- Remove skewers from water and add a piece of each veggie to the skewer. Leave a bit of room on the end of the skewers so they can be picked up easily.
- Barbeque on medium heat for a few minutes on each side until grill marks are visible on each side.

Oven Roasted Asparagus

Try substituting the sea salt with Herbamare Aromatic Sea Salt – a blend of savory spices and sea salt, available at your local health food store.

12 Servings	32 Servings	60 Servings	Ingredients
60 stems	160 stems	300 stems	Asparagus
6 Tbsp	1 cup	2 cups	Olive Oil
1 Tbsp	2 Tbsp	3 Tbsp	Sea Salt
1 Tbsp	2 Tbsp	3 Tbsp	Cracked Pepper
1 Tbsp	2 Tbsp	4 Tbsp	Lemon Juice
3 Tbsp	8 Tbsp	1 cup	Parmesan (fresh grated)

Directions:

- Remove the ends of the asparagus by breaking them off at the point where the asparagus end snaps off.
- Preheat oven to 375°F.
- Toss asparagus in olive oil, lemon juice, salt and pepper and layer in a casserole dish or 2 inch deep hotel insert.
- Grate parmesan and sprinkle on top of asparagus.
- Bake asparagus for 40 minutes or until soft enough to eat. Serve right away.

Grilled Green Beans with Slivered Almonds

Beans are served best when they are still a little crispy and hot! For a splash of flavor why not try jazzing them up with a splash of sambal oelek found at most large supermarkets – only add a bit as this condiment is quite spicy.

12 Servings	32 Servings	60 Servings	Ingredients
60 stems	160 stems	300 stems	Green Beans
6 Tbsp	1 cup	2 cups	Olive Oil or Garlic Butter
1 Tbsp	2 Tbsp	3 Tbsp	Sea Salt
1 Tbsp	2 Tbsp	3 Tbsp	Cracked Pepper
12 Tbsp	1 cup	2 cups	Slivered Almonds

Directions:

- Using a pair of sharp scissors cut the ends off the green beans.
- Heat oil or garlic butter on a flat top grill, toss green beans onto grill and sauté for a few moments.
- Sprinkle with sea salt and cracked pepper.
- Cook until just about tender. The beans should still have some crunch.
- Place into a 2 inch hotel pan and sprinkle with slivered almonds.

Option: Roast slivered almonds in an oven at 325°F until golden brown or about 20 minutes.

Variation: Add cooked spaghetti squash to the green beans after they are cooked or sauté julienned red peppers with the green beans for some added color.

Mac n' Cheese

A rich and cheesy dish with a nice crispy breadcrumb topping. An old time favorite!

12 Servings	32 Servings	60 Servings	Ingredients
6 cups	16 cups	30 cups	Uncooked Macaroni Noodles
2	3	4	Onions
¾ cup	1 ½ cups	2 ¼ cups	Butter/non-hydrogenated Margarine or Oil
9 Tbsp	1 cup	1 ½ cups	All-Purpose Flour
7 ½ cups	15 cups	45 cups	Sharp Cheddar Cheese
7 ½ cups	15 cups	45 cups	Milk
½ Tbsp	1 Tbsp	2 Tbsp	Sea Salt
½ Tbsp	1 Tbsp	2 Tbsp	Cracked Pepper
1 Tbsp	3 Tbsp	5 Tbsp	Worcestershire Sauce
1 Tbsp	3 Tbsp	5 Tbsp	Dry Mustard
1 Tbsp	3 Tbsp	5 Tbsp	Sweet Paprika
2	3	4	Bay Leaves
4 ½ cups	12 cups	22 cups	Bread Crumbs

Directions:

- Using a large stock pot, boil salted water and add macaroni noodles to boiling water.
- Stir every few minutes to prevent the noodles from sticking to the bottom of the pot and cook until slightly tender, about 20 minutes. The outside edges of the noodles should have turned white.
- Drain noodles reserving a few cups of the hot water to prevent the noodles from sticking together and set aside.
- In a large stock pot, melt butter or margarine over medium low heat and sauté onions until browned.
- Peel and slice onions in half and dice into small pieces. Grate cheese and set aside.
- Whisk flour into the above mixture and stir constantly until a thick paste has formed.

- Remove flour paste from heat, slowly add milk and mix until paste has dissolved.
- Over very low heat, add grated cheese (reserving 1/3 to sprinkle over top of casserole) to milk and slowly melt cheese. It is very important not to boil the milk as it will curdle.
- Stir constantly until cheese has melted, then add dry mustard, paprika, Worcestershire sauce, bay leaves and salt and pepper to taste.
- Preheat oven to 350°F and grease a large, 4 inch deep hotel insert. Add macaroni noodles, pour sauce over top of noodles and mix together. Spread bread crumbs over top of casserole and the remaining cheese.
- Bake for 40 minutes uncovered or until the top has browned and the macaroni is bubbling.

Roasted Carrots with Honey & Ginger

When roasting vegetables they tend to shrink considerably so I always go with a few extra, if there are left -overs they make a perfect addition to any soup.

12 Servings	32 Servings	60 Servings	Ingredients
18	48	90	Carrots
3 Tbsp	8 Tbsp	1 cup	Butter or non-hydrogenated Margarine
3 Tbsp	5 Tbsp	8 Tbsp	Ground Ginger
3 Tbsp	8 Tbsp	1 cup	Honey or Maple Syrup
1 Tbsp	2 Tbsp	3 Tbsp	Sea Salt
2 Tsp	1 Tbsp	2 Tbsp	Pepper

Directions:

- Preheat oven to 350°F.
- Peel and cut carrots into ¼ inch coins. Grease a large hotel insert and place carrots into greased pan.
- Add cubed butter or margarine pieces, honey or maple syrup and salt and pepper.
- Toss all ingredients together and cook for 50 minutes or until tender.
- ***Option:*** Instead of cutting carrots into coins, cut the carrots in half and then cut again crosswise into 2 inch long pieces and quarter again.

Roasted Maple Butternut Squash

A low fat side that tastes similar to pumpkin. Serve the squash in its skin and enjoy!

12 Servings	32 Servings	60 Servings	Ingredients
3	8	15	Butternut Squash
6 Tbsp	16 Tbsp	30 Tbsp	Butter or non-hydrogenated margarine
6 Tbsp	1 cup	2 cups	Maple Syrup
3 Tbsp	5 Tbsp	8 Tbsp	All Spice
1 Tbsp	3 Tbsp	5 Tbsp	Cinnamon
1 Tbsp	2 Tbsp	3 Tbsp	Sea Salt
2 tsp	1 Tbsp	2 Tbsp	Cracked Pepper

Directions:

- Preheat oven to 375°F.
- Place parchment on a large hotel sheet.
- Cut the squash in half and remove seeds and membranes.
- Place 1 Tbsp of butter or non-hydrogenated margarine in the center of each squash and sprinkle with allspice, cinnamon, salt and pepper. Cook for 75 – 90 minutes.
- Remove from oven and let cool slightly. Cut the squash halves in half and serve.

Roasted Spaghetti Squash with Butter

A healthy alternative to pasta... and it tastes delicious too!

12 Servings	32 Servings	60 Servings	Ingredients
6-8	16-18	30-32	Large Squash
6 Tbsp	1 cup	1 ¼ cup	Butter or non-hydrogenated Margarine
1 Tbsp	1 ½ Tbsp	2 Tbsp	Sea Salt
1 Tbsp	1 ½ Tbsp	2 Tbsp	Cracked Pepper

Directions:

- Preheat oven to 375°F.
- Slice the spaghetti squash in half and, using a fork or spoon, scoop the seeds out of the center and place the squash face down on a large hotel sheet with parchment placed underneath.
- Cook for 45 - 50 minutes, then turn the squash upright and cook for another half hour or until the squash feels soft to touch.
- Using a fork, scoop the spaghetti squash from its shell into a large pan.
- Toss with butter and salt and pepper to taste and place in oven. Keep warm until ready to serve.

Roasted Spaghetti Squash with Tomato Sauce & Parmesan

Makes a perfect vegan alternative to spaghetti just omit the parmesan and voila!

12 Servings	32 Servings	60 Servings	Ingredients
6-8	16-18	30-32	Large Squash
6 Tbsp	1 cup	1 ¼ cup	Butter or non-hydrogenated Margarine
1 Tbsp	1 ½ Tbsp	2 Tbsp	Sea Salt
1 Tbsp	1 ½ Tbsp	2 Tbsp	Cracked Pepper
3 cups	8 cups	15 cups	Tomato Sauce
1 ½ cups	2 cups	4 cups	Parmesan

Directions:

- Preheat oven to 375°F.
- Slice the spaghetti squash in half and, using a fork or spoon, scoop the seeds out of the center and place squash face down on a large hotel sheet with parchment placed underneath.
- Cook for 45 - 50 minutes, then turn the squash upright and cook for another half hour or until the squash feels soft to touch.
- Using a fork, scoop the spaghetti squash from its shell into a large pan.
- Toss with butter, tomato sauce and salt and pepper to taste. Sprinkle with grated parmesan cheese and place in oven. Keep warm until ready to serve.

Roasted Sweet Potatoes or Yams Fries

A popular dish that everyone loves… You can never make too many.

12 Servings	32 Servings	60 Servings	Ingredients
9	24	45	Sweet Potatoes or Yams
6 Tbsp	1 cup	1 ½ cups	Olive Oil
3 Tbsp	6 Tbsp	¾ cup	Sweet Paprika
3 Tbsp	6 Tbsp	¾ cup	Mrs. Dash Seasoning
2 Tbsp	4 Tbsp	6 Tbsp	Sea Salt (or to taste)
2 Tbsp	4 Tbsp	6 Tbsp	Cracked Pepper (or to taste)

Directions:

- Preheat oven to 375°F.
- Peel sweet potatoes or yams and slice in half through the middle and then again down the center of each half, cutting them in half. Take each half and slice into matchstick pieces.
- Toss the sweet potato or yam fries in oil, paprika, Mrs. Dash seasoning and salt and pepper to taste.
- Place parchment on a large hotel sheet (you may need more than one hotel sheet depending on the number of servings) and spread fries evenly on each sheet.
- Cook fries for 90 minutes or until soft on the inside and crunchy on the outside. Option: Combine sweet potato fries with potato wedges.

BBQ Corn on the Cob

Why not leave the husk on when barbequing - saves times and is a unique way of serving corn on the cob.

12 Servings	32 Servings	60 Servings	Ingredients
12	32	60	Large Corn

Directions:

- Prepare corn by placing in water about an hour before cooking. Remove any loose pieces of husk and cut off the fibers at the top of the ear.
- Preheat barbeque 15 minutes before cooking.
- Place soaked corn on the hot barbeque and cook for an hour (or more or less, depending on the temperature of your barbeque) over medium low heat, turning at least once.
- Remove from barbeque and place in a large hotel insert with lid on to keep warm until service.
- Serve with butter or get creative and make a flavored butter by adding minced cilantro or garlic.

Baked Potatoes

Use the baker's potatoes, and if they are quite large and you know the crowd you are serving won't eat a whole potato, cut the potatoes in half and use half as many.

12 Servings	32 Servings	60 Servings	Ingredients
12	32	60	Baker's Potatoes
12 Tbsp	1 cup	2 cups	Garlic Butter or Garlic & Herb Cream Cheese
3 Tbsp	¼ cup	½ cup	Coarse Salt

Directions:

- Preheat oven to 400°F.
- Wash potatoes and pat dry. Using a large serving fork stick fork into potatoes. Only need to do this once.
- Using a large cookie sheet or hotel pan, place parchment on sheet.
- Rub potatoes with garlic butter or garlic and herb cream cheese, place on the hotel pan and sprinkle with coarse salt. Bake for 90 minutes or until you can cut through the potato easily with a knife. Serve whole, or if the potatoes are quite big then cut in half.
- Serve with sour cream, minced chives or green onions and diced bacon bits.

Sour Cream & Garlic Mashed Potatoes

Boil the garlic cloves right in the pot with potatoes and mash into the potatoes. Make sure to leave those potato skins on, it saves time and the skins have all the nutrients.

12 Servings	32 Servings	60 Servings	Ingredients
20	60	100	Red or Brown Potatoes
6	12	24	Garlic cloves
6 Tbsp	1 cup	2 cups	Butter or Non-Hydrogenated Margarine
¾ cup	2 cups	3 ¼ cup	Milk
1 ½ cup	4 cups	7 cups	Sour Cream
½ Tbsp	1 Tbsp	2 Tbsp	Granulated Garlic Powder
1 Tbsp	3 Tbsp	5 Tbsp	Sea Salt (or to taste)
½ Tbsp	2 Tbsp	3 Tbsp	Cracked Pepper (or to taste)

Directions:

- In a large pot, place unpeeled quartered potatoes and peeled garlic cloves and fill with cold water. Add salt and bring to a boil.
- Boil potatoes until they are tender enough to pick up with a fork, and if they fall off of the fork right away they are done.
- Strain all but 1/3 of the water (this will help keep some of the flavor and help mash the potatoes) and add milk, butter or non-hydrogenated margarine, sour cream, granulated garlic powder and salt and pepper to taste.
- Mash potatoes with a large potato masher and then blend with a hand held mixer to help break up the garlic and create creamy potatoes.

Variation: Omit sour cream and garlic powder and substitute 1/3 the amount of peeled sweet potatoes for the potatoes. Replace sour cream with cream and butter.

Scalloped Potatoes

A rich and creamy dish with a crisp and cheesy topping.

12 Servings	32 Servings	60 Servings	Ingredients
18	48	90	Russet Potatoes or Red Potatoes
3	5	8	Large Onions
¾ cup	2 cups	4 cups	Butter or non-hydrogenated Margarine
¾ cup	2 cups	4 cups	All-Purpose Flour
1 Tbsp	3 Tbsp	5 Tbsp	Dried Mustard
1 Tbsp	3 Tbsp	5 Tbsp	Thyme
3 cups	8 cups	15 cups	Milk
1 Tbsp	3 Tbsp	5 Tbsp	Sea Salt
1 Tbsp	3 Tbsp	5 Tbsp	Pepper
3 cups	8 cups	15 cups	Parmesan
1 ½ cups	3 cups	5 cups	Shredded Cheddar Cheese

Directions:

- Slice potatoes very thinly and place into a large pot filled with cold water and salt and bring to a boil. Boil potatoes until slightly tender. Drain and set aside.
- Peel and slice onions in half and then slice again into thin strips.
- Preheat oven to 350°F, grease a large casserole pan or hotel insert and layer with potatoes, onions, 1/3 of the amount of flour, sprinkle with salt, pepper, thyme and ground mustard. Sprinkle with parmesan and add ¼ of the milk.
- Repeat layers until you have filled the casserole dish with the remaining ingredients. Top with the shredded cheddar cheese and bake for an hour or until the top has turned golden brown.

Variation: Omit the flour and add 1 - 340 ml can of condensed cream of mushroom soup for every serving 6 servings.

Pesto Penne

A simple dish and full of flavor… Just add the pesto to hot pasta and top with fresh grated parmesan cheese.

12 Servings	32 Servings	60 Servings	Ingredients
6 cups	16 cups	30 cups	Whole Wheat Penne
12 cups	32 cups	60 cups	Water
1 Tbsp	2 Tbsp	3 Tbsp	Sea Salt
3 cups	7 ½ cups	15 cups	Pesto
1 ½ cups	3 cups	5 cups	Parmesan (fresh grated)

Directions:

- In a large pot bring water to a boil and add salt and penne noodles. Cook until the noodles are al dente - about ½ an hour or until the edges of the noodles turn a whitish color. Strain noodles either by straining into a large colander or scooping out the noodles with a large strainer. Reserve a tiny bit of the water and do not rinse the noodles. The starch helps the sauce stick to the noodles and thicken it if need be. Pour a few tablespoons of the leftover hot pasta water or up to 1 cup, depending on the amount of servings you are preparing. Keep the noodles in their water to prevent them from sticking together.
- Follow Pesto recipe and add to the noodles. Top with freshly grated parmesan cheese.

Variation: Add cream to hot pasta and pesto for a pesto cream sauce.

Curried Vegetables & Chick Peas

A savoury side dish that uses clarified butter otherwise known as Ghee or try substituting coconut oil for a healthier option.

12 Servings	32 Servings	60 Servings	Ingredients
3	5	8	Onions
5-6 Tbsp	1 Cup	1 ½ Cups	Clarified Butter or Coconut oil
3	5	8	Zucchini
½	1 ½	3	Cauliflower Heads
3	5	8	Red Pepper
3	5	8	Green Pepper
1 250 ml	2 250 ml	4 250 ml	Canned Chick Peas
3-4 Tbsp	8-9 Tbsp	15-16 Tbsp	Mild Curry Paste
2 250 ml	4 250 ml	8 250 ml	Canned Coconut Milk
½ Cup	2 Cups	4 Cups	Yogurt
4	6	8	Cloves Minced Garlic
4-5 pieces	7-8 pieces	10-12 pieces	Ginger
1 Tbsp	2 Tbsp	3 Tbsp	Turmeric
1 Tbsp	3 Tbsp	5 Tbsp	Coriander
1 Tbsp	3 Tbsp	5 Tbsp	Cumin
3 Tbsp	8 Tbsp	1 Cup	Honey (or to taste)
1/2 tsp	1 1/2 Tsp	1 Tbsp	Sea salt (or to taste)

Directions:

- Peel onions and wash the other veggies.
- Dice onion, zucchini, cauliflower and red and green peppers into medium sized pieces.
- Peel and mince garlic and ginger.
- Sauté onions, cauliflower, garlic and ginger in clarified butter or coconut oil. Add turmeric, coriander, cumin, and curry paste.

- Add zucchini and peppers and sauté a couple of minutes.
- Drain and rinse Chickpeas and add to above mixture.
- Add coconut milk and yogurt and simmer until veggies are tender.
- Add honey and salt to taste.

MAIN DISHES

Paprika Breaded Pork Chops

Serve with garlic mashed potatoes or blended sweet potatoes & regular potatoes, roasted root vegetables or roasted maple syrup carrots, peas and apple sauce.

12 Servings	32 Servings	60 Servings	Ingredients
6 cups	16 cups	30 cups	Italian Style Bread Crumbs
5Tbsp	3/4 cup	1 1/2 cups	Sweet Paprika
18	48	90	Pork Chops (bone in)
9	24	45	Eggs
3 Tbsp	8 Tbsp	15 Tbsp	Milk
1 tsp	1 Tbsp	2 Tbsp	Sea Salt
1 tsp	1 Tbsp	2 Tbsp	Pepper

Directions:

- Prepare the bread crumb mixture according to the recipe in this book.
- Add paprika to bread crumb mixture. Crack eggs into a bowl and whisk until frothy, then add milk and salt and pepper.
- Dip fully thawed pork chops in egg mixture, dredge in bread crumb and paprika mixture, dip back into egg mixture and dredge again in bread crumb mixture for superb flavor. Bake at 350°F for an hour. Test with a meat thermometer to ensure it has been cooked to the appropriate temperature.

Salsa & Cheese Chicken

A simple and easy recipe for any crowd occasion.

12 Servings	32 Servings	60 Servings	Ingredients
12	32	60	Chicken Breasts
1 Tbsp	3 Tbsp	5 Tbsp	Sweet Paprika
1 tsp	1 Tbsp	3 Tbsp	Salt
1 tsp	1 Tbsp	3 Tbsp	Pepper
3 cups	8 cups	15 cups	Medium Salsa
1 ½ cups	4 cups	8 cups	Monterey Jack Cheese

Directions:

- Preheat oven to 375°F.
- Sprinkle salt, pepper and paprika on chicken and bake for 45 - 60 minutes.
- Grate cheese and set aside. ***Quick tip:*** When grating large amounts of cheese try using a food processor. Be sure to not overheat the processor by filling it too full with cheese.
- Remove chicken from oven, cover the top of each chicken breast with salsa and sprinkle with cheese. Bake until cheese melts. Serve immediately with Cajun rice, sautéed peppers and green beans.

Better Than Mom`s Lasagna

Not to brag or anything… but I have been told by many that my Lasagna is "better than mom`s" … Use oven-ready noodles to save time and cottage cheese rather than ricotta to save money.

12 Servings	32 Servings	60 Servings	Ingredients

Sauce:

3 kg	8 kg	15 kg	Ground Beef
3 Tbsp	8 Tbsp	12 Tbsp	Non-hydrogenated Oil
3	8	15	Onion
6-7 cloves	16-17 cloves	30-32 cloves	Garlic
2 each	6 each	12 each	Red/Green Peppers
3 stalks	8 stalks	12 stalks	Celery Rib and Leaves
1 kg	2 kg	3 kg	Mushrooms
1 – 1 L can	1 - 2.4 L can	2 - 2.4 L cans	Diced Tomatoes + Juice
1 156 ml	2 – 156 ml	4– 156 ml	Canned Tomato Paste
1 2.4 L	3 2.4 L	5 2.4 L	Tomato Sauce
1 1/2 cups	4 cups	7 cups	Parmesan Cheese
1 tsp	1 Tbsp	2 Tbsp	Sea Salt (or to taste)
1 tsp	1 Tbsp	2 Tbsp	Pepper (or to taste)
2 Tbsp	½ cup	1 cup	Chicken or Beef Stock (or to taste)
1 Tbsp	5 Tbsp	7 Tbsp	Sugar
2	4	6	Bay Leaves
2 Tbsp	6 Tbsp	10 Tbsp	Fresh or Dried Parsley
1 Tbsp	3 Tbsp	7 Tbsp	Thyme
1 Tbsp	3 Tbsp	7 Tbsp	Tarragon
1 ½ Tbsp	5 Tbsp	9 Tbsp	Basil
1 Tbsp	3 Tbsp	7 Tbsp	Oregano
1 tsp	1 Tbsp	3 Tbsp	Chilli Pepper Flakes
1 Tbsp	3 Tbsp	7 Tbsp	Worcestershire Sauce

Filling:

2 300 g packages	6 300 g packages	8 300 g packages	Frozen Spinach
5 cups	12 cups	22 cups	Cottage Cheese
1 1/2 cups	4 cups	7 cups	Parmesan Cheese
1 tsp	1 Tbsp	2 Tbsp	Sea Salt (or to taste)
1 tsp	1 Tbsp	2 Tbsp	Pepper (or to taste)
1 Tbsp	3 Tbsp	5 Tbsp	Crushed Fennel
1½ 375 g packages	3-4 375 g pkgs	5-6 375 g pkgs	Oven Ready Lasagna Noodles
3 cups	8 cups	15 cups	Shredded Mozzarella and Cheddar Cheese

Directions:

- Heat oil in a large rondeau and cook ground beef until almost fully cooked. Drain off most of the fat, add diced onions to the meat and sauté until onions are translucent. Add minced garlic, dried oregano, thyme, tarragon, parsley, basil and chili pepper flakes.
- Wash and cut peppers in half, remove membrane and dice the peppers. Wash and dice celery into small pieces and cut washed mushrooms into quarters. Add diced peppers, celery and celery rib and mushrooms to sauce.
- Add tomato sauce, diced tomatoes, tomato paste, parmesan, more garlic and spices if needed, stock and salt and pepper to taste. Simmer until flavors merge.
- Thaw frozen spinach and drain any excess liquid. Add spinach to cottage cheese. Using a pestle and mortar grind fennel and add to cottage cheese mixture. Add parmesan, salt and pepper.
- Grate mozzarella and cheddar cheese and set aside.
- In a large greased casserole dish or 4 inch deep hotel pan, layer a quarter of the sauce, then the noodles, then cottage cheese, then a layer of grated mozzarella cheddar and repeat.
- Finish with a layer of shredded mozza, cheddar, a sprinkle of parmesan and dried parsley.
- Cover the pan with a layer of plastic wrap and foil to prevent cheeses from burning. Note: The plastic wrap will help prevent the foil from breaking down and leaving foil spots on the food. Always cover plastic wrap with tin foil.
- Bake in a preheated oven at 375°F for an hour and twenty mintues. Remove foil and plastic wrap for the last 10 minutes to melt the cheese. Let cool slightly and cut into 2 x 2 inch pieces.

Two-Sauce Roasted Vegetable Lasagna

This lasagna can be either served with a traditional béchamel sauce or a simple tomato sauce.

12 Servings	32 Servings	60 Servings	Ingredients
1½ - 375g packages	5 - 375 g pkgs	9 - 375 pkgs	Oven Ready Lasagna Noodles
2	3	4	Red Onion
3	5	8	Carrots
3	5	8	Zucchini
3	5	8	Red Peppers
1	2	3	Eggplant
5 Tbsp	9 Tbsp	¼ cup	Olive Oil
5 cups	12 cups	22 cups	Cottage Cheese
2 - 300g packages	4 - 300g pkgs	8 - 300g pkgs	Frozen Spinach
2 Tbsp	3 Tbsp	5 Tbsp	Crushed Fennel
¾ cup	2 cups	7 cups	Feta (optional)
½ Tbsp	1 ½ Tbsp	2 Tbsp	Sea Salt (or to taste)
½ Tbsp	1 ½ Tbsp	2 Tbsp	Pepper (or to taste)
3 cups	12 cups	22 ½ cups	Mozzarella

Tomato Sauce

12 Servings	32 Servings	60 Servings	Ingredients
1 - 2.4L can	2 - 2.4 L cans	3 - 2.4 L cans	Crushed Tomatos
1 156 ml	2 156 ml	3 156 ml	Tomato Paste
1 - 1L can	1 - 2.4 L can	2 - 2.4 L can	Diced Tomatoes + Juice
3 Tbsp	8 Tbsp	1 cup	Crushed Garlic
3 Tbsp	5 Tbsp	8 Tbsp	Oregano
3 Tbsp	5 Tbsp	8 Tbsp	Tarragon
3 Tbsp	5 Tbsp	8 Tbsp	Thyme
3 Tbsp	5 Tbsp	8 Tbsp	Basil
1 Tbsp	2 Tbsp	3 Tbsp	Sea Salt (or to taste)
1 Tbsp	2 Tbsp	3 Tbsp	Pepper (or to taste)
1 ½ Tbsp	3 Tbsp	5 Tbsp	Sugar

¾ cup	2 cups	3 ¾ cups	Parmesan
2	4	6	Bay Leaves

Béchamel Sauce

7 ½ cups	20 cups	37 ½ cups	Milk
7	15	25	Crushed Garlic Cloves
12 Tbsp	1 ¼ cup	2 cups	Butter
1 ½ cups	4 cups	7 cups	Cream
1 Tbsp	3 Tbsp	5 Tbsp	Vegetable Stock
½ Tbsp	2 Tbsp	3 Tbsp	Nutmeg
2	3	4	Bay Leaves
3 cups	8 cups	15 cups	Parmesan

Directions:

- Thaw spinach either by placing in the fridge overnight or at room temperature a few hours before using. Drain spinach thoroughly before adding to cottage cheese by squeezing out any excess water with your hands.
- Prepare sauce by combining crushed tomato sauce, paste, diced canned tomatoes, minced garlic, spices, salt and pepper, bay leaves and parmesan. Simmer sauce until the flavors merge.
- If using oven-ready lasagna noodles then have ready, otherwise boil regular noodles in salted water, drain and let cool.
- Slice zucchini, eggplant and carrot lengthwise into large pieces. Julienne red pepper and dice onion into medium-sized pieces. Coat vegetables in oil, sprinkle with sea salt and roast in a large baking dish for 20 minutes or until the outsides are just browned. You don't want them to be fully cooked through.
- Crush fennel with a mortar and pestle.
- Mix cottage cheese, thawed spinach, crushed fennel seeds and salt and pepper. Option: Add feta for a different flavor.
- Shred mozzarella and set aside.
- In a large casserole dish or hotel pan layer lasagne starting with a 1/3 cup of sauce, then a layer of noodles, then a layer of cottage cheese mixture, followed by a layer of roasted vegetables and repeat layers.
- Top with a nice thick layer of mozza, parmesan and fresh chopped parsley.
- Preheat oven to 375°F and bake until cheese has melted and is golden brown.

Chicken Fajitas

Serve this mouthwatering dish with rice, refried beans, stir-fried peppers and onions, sour cream, grated cheddar cheese, salsa and guacamole.

12 Servings	32 Servings	60 Servings	Ingredients
8	24	45	Chicken Breasts
3	8	15	Red Peppers
3	8	15	Green Peppers
3	8	15	Onions
6 cloves	9 cloves	12 cloves	Garlic
1 40 g package	1½-2 40 g pkgs	2½-3 40 g pkgs	Fajita Seasoning (or to taste)
1 Tbsp	5 Tbsp	7 Tbsp	Tabasco Seasoning or Hot Sauce
1 Tbsp	5 Tbsp	7 Tbsp	Cumin
1 small	3 small	5 small	Green Chili Peppers
3	7	9	Squeezed Limes
3 Tbsp	8 Tbsp	¼ cup	Oil
1cup	2 1/2 cups	5 cups	Water
1 tsp	½ Tbsp	1 Tbsp	Sea Salt (or to taste)

Directions:

- Wash the peppers, cut in half and remove the membrane. Julienne the peppers, onions and chicken.
- Crush the garlic cloves and mince.
- Over medium-low heat in a large rondeau, sauté chicken in oil until tender. Add garlic, fajita seasoning and water.
- Add peppers, tabasco seasoning or hot sauce, cumin, lime juice and salt.
- Sauté until peppers and onions are soft.
- Serve with whole wheat tortillas, Mexican rice with black beans, refried beans, shredded Tex Mex or Montery Jack cheese, guacamole, sour cream and salsa.

Beef & Bean Burritos

An old time favorite...that never grows old.

12 Servings	32 Servings	60 Servings	Ingredients
3 kg	8 kg	15 kg	Ground Beef
3 cups	8 cups	15 cups	Black Beans
2	5	9	Onions
8 cloves	15 cloves	24 cloves	Garlic
4 Tbsp	8 Tbsp	12 Tbsp	Vegetable Oil
1 - 40 g package	1 ½ - 40 g packages	3 - 40 g packages	Low Sodium Burrito Seasoning
2	4	6	Fresh Green chilies (minced)
¾ cup	2 ½ cups	5 cups	Water
2 Tbsp	5 Tbsp	8 Tbsp	Cumin
1 Tbsp	3 Tbsp	5 Tbsp	Chili Powder or Hot Sauce to taste
1 Tbsp	3 Tbsp	5 Tbsp	Chicken or Beef Stock

Directions:

- In a large rondeau, sauté ground beef over medium heat until beef is cooked and drain off any fat, reserving only a couple of tablespoons.
- Finely dice garlic, chilies (deseed first) and onions. Add to ground beef mixture and sauté until onions are tender. Note: When deseeding chilies use gloves, or if gloves are not available then use the side of your knife, pulling the seeds away from you. Do not use your hands or the heat from the chili will transfer to your skin and will burn!
- Add burrito seasoning, cumin, hot sauce and stock.
- Drain and rinse black beans and add to beef mixture.
- Add water if beef mixture seems too dry.
- Wrap with whole wheat wraps and serve with your favorite Mexican toppings such as Mexican rice, guacamole, salsa, shredded cheese and sour cream.

Vegetarian Option: Substitute ground textured soy meat for ground beef available at your local supermarket and cook according to instructions on package. Add the same ingredients as above. Use veggie stock instead of chicken or beef.

Beef Tacos

For a vegetarian option simply omit the beef and substitute with Taco flavored Ground Round, a textured soy product that is quite delicious even a meat eater would have a hard time telling the difference.

12 Servings	32 Servings	60 Servings	Ingredients
3 kg	8 kg	15 kg	Ground Beef
3	7	12	Onions
8 cloves	15 cloves	24 cloves	Garlic
Tbsp	8 Tbsp	12 Tbsp	Vegetable Oil
1 - 40 g package	2 - 40 g package	3 - 40 g packages	Low Sodium Taco Seasoning
2 minced	4 minced	8 minced	Fresh Green chilies
½ cup	1 cups	1 ½ cups	Water
2 Tbsp	4 Tbsp	6 Tbsp	Cumin
1 Tbsp	3 Tbsp	5 Tbsp	Chili Powder or Hot Sauce (or to taste)*
1 Tbsp	3 Tbsp	5 Tbsp	Chicken or Beef Stock

Directions:

- Sauté ground beef over medium heat until beef is cooked and drain off any fat, reserving 1/4 to prevent the beef from drying out.
- Finely dice garlic, chilies (deseed first) and onions; add to ground beef mixture and sauté until onions are tender. Note: When deseeding chilies use gloves, or if gloves are not available then use the side of your knife, pulling the seeds away from you. Do not use your hands or the heat from the chili will transfer to your skin and will burn!
- Add taco seasoning, cumin, hot sauce and stock.
- Drain and rinse black beans and add to beef mixture.
- Add water to help the beef from drying out as it cooks.
- Serve in warmed tacos and add your favorite toppings such as diced tomatoes, shredded lettuce, diced onions, shredded Tex Mex or Monterey Jack cheese, guacamole, salsa and sour cream.

Vegetarian Option: Use Ground Round from your local super market and cook according to instructions on package. Add the same ingredients as above. Use veggie stock instead of chicken or beef.

Spaghetti

Serve with warmed garlic toast, Caesar salad and a sprinkle of parmesan cheese. The longer you can let the sauce simmer, the more flavorful this dish will be!

12 Servings	32 Servings	60 Servings	Ingredients
3 kg	8 kg	15 kg	Ground Beef
3 Tbsp	9 Tbsp	1 cup	Olive Oil or non-hydrogenated Canola Oil
3	5	8	Large Onions
6 -7 cloves	16 -17 cloves	30-32 cloves	Minced Garlic
2 each	5 each	8 each	Red and Green Peppers
3 stalks	1 whole	2 whole	Celery Rib & Leaves
3	8	12	Carrots
1é2 kg	2.5 kg	4 kg	Fresh Mushrooms
1 540 ml	1 2.4 L	2 2.4 L	Diced Tomatoes + juice
1 -156 ml can	2 -156 ml cans	4 – 156 ml cans	Tomato Paste
1 - 2.4 L can	3 - 2.4 L	cans	5 - 2.4 L cans Tomato Sauce
1 ½ cups	3 cups	5 cups	Parmesan Cheese
1 tsp	1 Tbsp	2 Tbsp	Sea Salt (or to taste)
1 tsp	1 Tbsp	2 Tbsp	Pepper (or to taste)
2 Tbsp	½ cup	1 cup	Chicken or Beef Stock
1 Tbsp	2 Tbsp	3 Tbsp	Sugar
2 tsp	2 Tbsp	3 Tbsp	Celery Seed
3	5	7	Bay Leaves
1 Tbsp	3 Tbsp	5 Tbsp	Fresh or Dried Parsley
1 Tbsp	3 Tbsp	5 Tbsp	Tarragon
1 Tbsp	3 Tbsp	5 Tbsp	Thyme
1 ½ Tbsp	4 Tbsp	6 Tbsp	Basil
1 Tbsp	3 Tbsp	5 Tbsp	Oregano

1 Tbsp	3 Tbsp	5 Tbsp	Cumin
1 tsp	3 tsp	5 tsp	Chilli Pepper Flakes
1 Tbsp	3 Tbsp	5 Tbsp	Worcestershire Sauce
18 cups(1.5 kg dry)	48 cups(2.5 kg dry)	90 cups(5 kg dry)	Cooked Spaghetti Noodles

Directions:

- In a large rondeau, heat oil and sauté beef until just fully cooked and drain off any excess fat, reserving about 1/3 of the fat.
- Finely mince garlic cloves and peel onions and dice into small pieces. Add minced garlic and diced onions to the beef mixture and cook until onions are soft.
- Peel and medium-dice carrots and celery and quarter washed mushrooms. Add to above ingredients and sauté for a few minutes.
- Wash and slice peppers in half, remove the membrane and dice into bite-size pieces.
- Add tomato sauce, paste, diced tomatoes and juice, diced peppers, parmesan cheese, stock, salt and pepper to taste, sugar, celery seed, bay leaves, parsley, basil, thyme, oregano, tarragon, cumin, chili pepper flakes and Worcestershire sauce. Simmer ingredients until the flavors merge and adjust seasoning to taste.
- Using a large stock pot, boil salted water and add spaghetti noodles to boiling water. Stir every few minutes to prevent the noodles from sticking to the bottom of the pot and cook until slightly tender, about 20 minutes. Drain noodles reserving a few cups of the hot water to prevent the noodles from sticking together and set aside.
- Test doneness by throwing a noodle to the wall to see if it sticks. If it does it means it is done – this trick really does work! Strain noodles from pasta water and reserve a bit of water to add to noodles to prevent noodles from sticking together, or add spaghetti sauce to the noodles and mix together.

Parmesan Breaded Chicken with Black Olive Tomato Sauce

An Italian inspired favorite with crispy parmesan outside, served with a savory tomato and black olive sauce and topped with a hearty layer of fresh mozza.

12 Servings	32 Servings	60 Servings	Ingredients
12	32	60	Chicken Breasts
6 cups	16 cups	30 cups	Italian Bread Crumbs
3 cups	5 cups	9 cups	Parmesan
6	16	30	Eggs
½ cup	1 cup	1 ½ cup	Milk
1 Tsp	½ Tbsp	1 Tbsp	Sea Salt
1 Tsp	½ Tbsp	1 Tbsp	Pepper
1 ¼ cups	3 cups	5 cups	Black Olives
1 1L	1 2.4 L	2 2.4 L	Tomato Sauce
1 – 156 ml	2 156 ml	3 156 ml	Canned Tomato Paste
3 Tbsp	5 Tbsp	9 Tbsp	Red Wine Vinegar
2	3	5	Onions
6 cloves	12 cloves	18 cloves	Minced Garlic
1 Tbsp	3 Tbsp	5 Tbsp	Oregano
1 Tbsp	2 Tbsp	3 Tbsp	Chicken Stock
2 tsp	1 Tbsp	2 Tbsp	Garlic Powder
2	3	5	Bay Leaves
1 Tbsp	3 Tbsp	5 Tbsp	Basil
1 Tbsp	3 Tbsp	5 Tbsp	Ground Sage
1 Tbsp	3 Tbsp	5 Tbsp	Marjoram
1 Tbsp	2 Tbsp	3 Tbsp	Lemon Juice
1 Tbsp	2 Tbsp	3 Tbsp	Sugar
¾ cup	1 ½ cups	3 cups	Shredded Parmesan or Mozzarella

Directions:

- Prepare the sauce by peeling onions and garlic and mince. Heat olive oil in a large stock pot. Add onions and garlic to oil as well as basil and oregano and sauté on low heat until the onions are soft.
- Drain black olives, dice and set aside.
- Add red wine vinegar to softened onions and sauté until lightly browned.
- Add tomato sauce, tomato paste, parmesan, garlic powder, and lemon juice. Add bay leaves, diced black olives and chicken stock. Simmer sauce for about an hour or until the flavors merge.
- Mix dried parmesan with the Italian bread crumbs and set aside. Crack eggs into a large bowl and mix with a fork until the yolks are broken. Combine eggs and milk together and add a dash of salt and pepper.
- Meanwhile, bread chicken by dredging in parmesan Italian bread crumbs, dipping in the egg and milk mixture and dredging again in the breadcrumb mixture.
- Preheat oven to 375°F. Place chicken breasts on large hotel pan or cookie sheet with parchment placed underneath and bake for 45 minutes. Remove from oven, add sauce to cover the chicken breasts, sprinkle with parmesan and bake until cheese has melted.
- Serve with Roasted Garlic and Sundried Tomato Fettuccine or Fettuccine Alfredo and sautéed green beans.

Chicken Souvlaki

A zesty lemony flavour and don`t forget all the fixings to serve on the side!

12 Servings	32 Servings	60 Servings	Ingredients
18	48	90	Chicken Breasts
3 cups	5 cups	7 cups	Olive Oil or non-hydrogenated Oil
1 ½ cups	3 cups	5 cups	Lemon Juice
6 Tbsp	½ cup	1 cup	Minced Garlic
1 Tbsp	3 Tbsp	5 Tbsp	Sweet Paprika
3 Tbsp	5 Tbsp	7 Tbsp	Oregano
3 Tbsp	5 Tbsp	7 Tbsp	Basil
1 Tbsp	3 Tbsp	5 Tbsp	Thyme
1 Tbsp	3 Tbsp	5 Tbsp	Sugar
1 tsp	1 Tbsp	2 Tbsp	Salt
1 tsp	1 Tbsp	2 Tbsp	Pepper
24	64	120	Skewers (optional)

Directions:

- Prepare marinade by combining oil, lemon juice, minced garlic, paprika, oregano, basil, thyme, salt, sugar and pepper.
- Dice chicken breasts into small cubes and place in a 4 inch deep hotel pan. Marinade chicken for a couple of hours in the Greek marinade.
- You may cook the chicken pieces as is, or if you want to serve on a skewer, then spear 5 to 6 pieces on each skewer and place skewers in a shallow hotel pan. Slowly cook in preheated oven at 325°F for 90 minutes or until done.
- Serve with roasted greek lemon potatoes or lemon rice, diced tomatoes, cucumbers, onions and lettuce in warm pitas with tzatziki and humus on the side.

Variation: Substitute pork for chicken. You can either buy pre-diced pork or use 1 large pork-loin for every 12 servings.

Eggplant or Zucchini Parmesan

Whether you are vegetarian or not this dish is very delightful and filling!

12 Servings	32 Servings	60 Servings	Ingredients
6 cups	16 cups	30 cups	Italian Bread crumbs
3	7	12	Eggplant or Zucchini (double the amount if using zucchini)
6	16	30	Eggs
1/2 cup	1 1/2 cups	3 cups	Milk
6 cups	16 cups	24 cups	Parmesan
1 - 1L can	1 - 2.4 L can	2 - 2.4 L cans	Tomato Sauce
1 - 6oz can	2 - 6oz cans	3 - 6oz cans	Tomato Paste
1 Tbsp	3 Tbsp	5 Tbsp	Red Wine Vinegar
3 cloves	8 cloves	12 cloves	Minced Garlic
1 Tbsp	5 Tbsp	7 Tbsp	Sugar
3 Tbsp	5 Tbsp	8 Tbsp	Basil
3 Tbsp	5 Tbsp	8 Tbsp	Oregano
3 Tbsp	5 Tbsp	8 Tbsp	Ground Sage
3 Tbsp	5 Tbsp	8 Tbsp	Marjoram
3 Tbsp	5 Tbsp	8 Tbsp	Basil Leaves
1 Tbsp	3 Tbsp	5 Tbsp	Salt
1 Tbsp	2 Tbsp	3 Tbsp	Pepper
3 cups	8 cups	15 cups	Mozzarella

Directions:

- Prepare sauce by combining minced garlic, tomato sauce, tomato paste, red wine vinegar, sugar, basil, oregano, ground sage, marjoram and 1/2 the amount of parmesan. Bring to a simmer until the flavours merge. Add salt and pepper to taste.
- If using eggplant, slice lengthwise into ¼ inch pieces, sprinkle with salt and let sit on baking sheet for 20 minutes. This draws out any bitterness in the eggplant. With a paper towel pat off the salt and any juices that emerge.

- Combine eggs, milk, and half the amount of salt and pepper together. Dip eggplant or zuchinni in bread crumb mixture, then in egg mixture and dip into breadcrumb mixture again. Bake at 375°F for 12 – 15 minutes. ***Optional:*** Pan fry the breaded eggplant or zuchinni in oil for a crispy outside and then follow the instructions below.
- Layer sauce on top of eggplant or zucchini and then a layer of mozzarella and parmesan. Bake again until cheese is slightly browned.
- Serve with egg noodles or rice, garlic toast, stir fried green beans and Caesar Salad.

Stuffed Zucchini

This wonderfully scrumptious dish can be served as side dish or as a main.

12 Servings	32 Servings	60 Servings	Ingredients
12	32	60	Zucchini
2 cups	5 cups	10 cups	Italian Style Bread Crumbs
3	5	8	Eggs
6 cups	15 cups	30 cups	Cottage Cheese
1 cup	3 cups	5 cups	Soft Tofu
1 Tbsp	2 Tbsp	3 Tbsp	Onion Powder
1 Tbsp	3 Tbsp	5 Tbsp	Oregano
1 Tbsp	3 Tbsp	5 Tbsp	Thyme
1 Tbsp	3 Tbsp	5 Tbsp	Fennel
1 Tbsp	3 Tbsp	5 Tbsp	Parsley
½ Tbsp	1 ½ Tbsp	2 Tbsp	Sea Salt (or to taste)
½ Tbsp	1 ½ Tbsp	2 Tbsp	Pepper (or to taste)
3 cups	8 cups	15 cups	Parmesan

Directions:

- Wash and cut zucchini in half and then slice lengthwise down the middle to make two halves.
- Using a spoon, scoop out the middle of the zucchini to remove the seeds.
- Mix cottage cheese, soft tofu, eggs, bread crumbs, spices and ¾ cup of parmesan cheese. Add salt and pepper to taste.
- Stuff the hollowed out part of the zucchini with the cheese mixture.
- Top with leftover parmesan cheese.
- Bake at 350°F for 20 minutes or until the top of cheese mixture is golden brown.

Chipotle Chilli

Such a satisfying meal with a secret ingredient using cocoa…

12 Servings	32 Servings	60 Servings	Ingredients
3 kg	8 kg	15 kg	Ground Beef
3	5	8	Onions
3	7	12	Carrots
3 stalks	8 stalks	15 stalks	Celery and rib
3	5	8	Green Peppers
3	5	8	Red Peppers
1 cup	3 cups	5 cups	Frozen Corn
1 - 250 ml cans	3 - 250 ml cans	5 - 250 ml cans	Kidney beans
1 - 250 ml cans	2 - 250 ml can	3 - 250 ml cans	Garbanzo Beans
6-7 cloves	8-10 cloves	12-14 cloves	Garlic
3 Tbsp	8 Tbsp	12 Tbsp	Olive Oil
2 - 540 ml cans	4 - 540 ml cans	6 - 540 ml cans	Diced Tomatoes + Juice
2 - 796 ml cans	2 - 2.84 L cans	3 - 2.84 L can	Tomato Purée or Sauce
1 - 196 ml can	2 - 196 ml cans	3 - 196 ml cans	Tomato Paste
3 Tbsp	7 Tbsp	10 Tbsp	Tabasco Sauce
6 Tbsp	12 Tbsp	15 Tbsp	Chilli Powder (or to taste)
2 tsp	2 Tbsp	3 Tbsp	Flaked Chilli Peppers
1 Tbsp	2 Tbsp	3 Tbsp	Chipotle Peppers or Liquid Smoke (or to taste)
1 Tbsp	3 Tbsp	5 Tbsp	Chicken or Beef Stock
1 Tbsp	5 Tbsp	9 Tbsp	Cumin
11/2 Tbsp	5 Tbsp	7 Tbsp	Cocoa
1 Tbsp	3 Tbsp	5 Tbsp	Worcestershire Sauce
3	4	5	Bay Leaves

Directions:

- In a large rondeau, heat oil and sauté beef until almost fully cooked. Remove from heat, let cool slightly, strain the majority of the fat and return to heat.
- Peel and dice onions into small pieces. Remove outer layer of the garlic and mince. Add onions and garlic to beef and sauté until the onions are soft.
- Slice peppers in half, remove membrane and dice into small cubes. Set aside.
- Add chili powder, cumin, cocoa, chili peppers, tabasco, chipotle peppers or liquid smoke, stock, bay leaves and salt and pepper. Adjust seasoning to taste. If using chipotle peppers make sure to wear gloves when removing the seeds and membranes, and do not touch your eyes! Sautee for a few minutes.
- Add frozen corn, tomato paste, tomato sauce, diced tomatoes and juice, rinsed beans and diced peppers.
- Simmer chilli for an hour or more. The longer you simmer it, the better it will taste! Serve with Jalapeno Corn Bread and Mexican Rice.

Vegetarian Chilli with TVP

TVP is textured vegetable protein that has come a long way since I first experienced with this product. I have found Bob`s Red Mill TVP to be the best product in terms of taste.

12 Servings	32 Servings	60 Servings	Ingredients
3	5	8	Onions
3	8	15	Carrots
1	2	3	Zucchinis
3 Stalks	8 Stalks	15 Stalks	Celery and rib
3	8	15	Green Peppers
3	8	15	Red peppers
2 cups	4 cups	8 cups	Acorn Squash, Butternut squash or Yams
2 - 250 ml cans	4 - 250 ml cans	6 - 250 ml cans	Kidney Beans
1 - 250 ml cans	2 - 250 ml can	3 - 250 ml cans	Garbanzo Beans
6-7 cloves	8-10 cloves	12-14 cloves	Garlic
3 Tbsp	6 Tbsp	8 Tbsp	Olive Oil
1/2 cup	1 1/2 cups	3 cups	TVP
1 - 796 ml can	1 - 2.4 L can	2 - 2.4 L cans	Diced Tomatoes +Juice
2 - 796 ml cans	1 - 2.4 L can	2 - 2.4 L cans	Tomato Sauce
1 cup	3 cups	5 cups	Tomato Juice
6 Tbsp	12 Tbsp	15 Tbsp	Chilli Powder (or to taste)
2 tsp	3 tsp	4 tsp	Flaked Chilli Peppers
1 Tbsp	2 Tbsp	3 Tbsp	Chipotle Peppers or Liquid Smoke (or to taste)
1 Tbsp	3 Tbsp	5 Tbsp	Vegetarian Stock
2 Tbsp	5 Tbsp	9 Tbsp	Cumin
1 Tbsp	3 Tbsp	5 Tbsp	Cocoa
1 Tbsp	3 Tbsp	5 Tbsp	Worcestershire Sauce
3	4	6	Bay Leaves

Directions:

- Peel onions and squash or yams, dice into bite-sized pieces and set aside. Peel and mince garlic. In a large stock pot, heat oil and sauté squash, onions and garlic until soft.
- Peel and dice carrots into medium-sized pieces and add to sautéing vegetables. Slice peppers, remove the membrane and dice into ½ inch pieces. Wash and dice zucchini into small pieces.
- Heat water in a kettle and add a few tablespoons to the TVP and fluff with a fork.
- Once sautéing vegetables are somewhat soft, add tomato sauce, diced tomatoes and tomato juice, zucchini and rinsed beans. Add the peppers and TVP.
- Add cumin, cocoa, chili powder, salt and pepper, vegetarian stock, chili peppers and bay leaves. Adjust seasoning to taste.

Enchiladas

Serve with beef or chicken, and if making vegetarian enchiladas, simply omit meat and add more veggies and refried beans.

12 Servings	32 Servings	60 Servings	Ingredients
3 Tbsp	5 Tbsp	8 Tbsp	Olive oil
3 kg	8 kg	15 kg	Ground Beef
2	6	12	Onion
3	8	15	Red Peppers
3	8	15	Green Peppers
6-7	10-12	15-18	Garlic Cloves
1 - 40 g package	2 - 40 g package	3 - 40 g packages	Fajita Seasoning
2 Tbsp	5 Tbsp	7 Tbsp	Cumin
1 Tsp	1 Tbsp	2 Tbsp	Sea Salt (or to taste)
1 Tsp	1 Tbsp	2 Tbsp	Pepper (or to taste)
2 Tbsp	5 Tbsp	10 Tbsp	Green Chillies
3 Tbsp	5 Tbsp	8 Tbsp	Tabasco Sauce
5 cups	12 cups	23 cups	Refried Beans

Sauce:

8 cups (2 796 ml)	24 cups (2 2.84 L)	45 cups (3 2.84 L)	Tomato Purée
2 - 540 ml cans	1 - 2.4 L can	2 - 2.4 L cans	Diced Tomatoes plus juice
1 Tbsp	3 Tbsp	5 Tbsp	Oregano
3 cups	8 cups	15 cups	Heavy Cream
3 Tbsp	8 Tbsp	15 Tbsp	Cilantro
3 Tbsp	8 Tbsp	15 Tbsp	Garlic Clove
1 Tsp	1 Tbsp	2 Tbsp	Sea Salt (or to taste)
1 Tsp	1 Tbsp	2 Tbsp	Pepper (or to taste)
18	48	90	8" Whole Wheat and/ or White Tortillas
4 ½ cups	22 ½ cups	48 cups	Monterey Jack Cheddar Cheese (grated)

Directions:

- First prepare the sauce by combining tomato purée, heavy cream, minced garlic, oregano, cilantro and salt and pepper to taste. Simmer until the flavors merge.
- In a large pot, heat refried beans and purée beans so the consistency is smooth. Sometimes I add a few chillies in with the beans to spice them up. You can make your own, but canned refried beans are just as yummy and easier.
- Heat oil in a large rondeau and sauté the lean ground beef until almost fully cooked. Drain off most of the fat, reserving just a bit to prevent the meat from drying out. As the meat is sautéing, julienne onions and bell peppers, removing the membranes from the peppers.
- Sauté onions in with meat until soft. Then add peppers, minced garlic, tabasco sauce, cumin, fajita seasoning and chilli pepper. Set aside mixture and let cool.
- To assemble enchiladas, pour a layer of sauce on the bottom of a large casserole dish or 2 inch deep hotel pan.
- Spoon meat mixture into centre of tortilla, layer with refried beans and sprinkle 2 Tbsp of cheese on top.
- Roll the enchiladas by folding the edge over the ingredients in the middle, then fold the sides inwards, roll the enchilada away from you and place seam side down in casserole dish.
- Repeat with remaining tortillas.
- Spoon remaining sauce over the enchiladas, top with remaining cheese.
- Bake for 25 minutes until hot and bubbly.

Chunky Jambalaya

Yummmmmm……. Use a nice spicy chorizo sausage and cayenne pepper to make this dish pop!

12 Servings	32 Servings	60 Servings	Ingredients
4 Slices	1/2 500 g Pack	1 500 g Packs	Bacon (finely diced)
14 - 16	28 - 32	58 - 62	Prawns
14 - 16	28 - 32	58 - 62	Scallops
2	4	6	Chorizo Sausage or Italian Sausage
6	12	24	Chicken Breast
3	6	12	Onion
4	8	16	Green Bell Peppers
3	5	12	Red Bell Peppers
3 Stalks	10 Stalks	18 Stalks	Celery
6	12	18	Garlic Cloves
7 ½ cups	15 cups	30 cups	Parboiled Rice
11 cups	22 ½ cups	45 cups	Water
¼ cup	¾ cup	1 cup	Chicken Stock
1 Tbsp	3 Tbsp	5 Tbsp	Butter or non-hydro-genated Margarine
2 - 540 ml cans	1 - 2.4 L can	2 - 2.4 L can	Diced Tomatoes
2 - 156 ml cans	3 - 156 ml cans	4 - 156 ml cans	Tomato Paste
1 ½ cups	5 cups	8 cups	Tomato Juice
3 cups	6 cups	10 cups	Black Beans
3 cups	8 cups	12 cups	Salsa
3 Tbsp	5 Tbsp	7 Tbsp	Tabasco
1 Tsp	1 Tbsp	2 Tbsp	Cayenne Pepper (or to taste)
2	5	10	Fresh Limes
1 ¼ tsp	1 Tbsp	2 Tbsp	Sea Salt (or to taste)
1 ¼ tsp	1 Tbsp	2 Tbsp	Cracked Pepper (or to taste)

2	3	7	Bay leaves
1 Tbsp	3 Tbsp	5 Tbsp	Thyme

Directions:

- Preheat oven to 350°F. Measure parboiled rice into a greased 8 inch hotel insert and add water, chicken stock, butter or non-hydrogenated margarine, tomato paste and diced tomatoes plus their juice.
- Cover rice with plastic wrap and tinfoil and cook rice for about 90 minutes.
- Meanwhile, dice sausage, bacon and chicken into bite-sized pieces. Heat oil in a large frying pan and sauté chicken until browned on the outside; add chorizo and bacon and sauté until the meat is cooked all the way through. Remove meat from pan and set aside, but save the juices from the meat.
- Heat the juice from the meat. If there is too much grease from the bacon you can ladle the grease off the top. (Be sure to dispose of it either in a metal can or glass jar, not down the drain.) Add the minced garlic and onions and sauté for a couple of minutes or until the onions become translucent. The other option is to partially cook the bacon in the oven first to remove some of grease, and then let it cool and dice into medium-sized pieces.
- Wash and dice the sweet bell peppers, removing the membrane and seeds. Wash and dice celery, add to the sautéing onions and garlic and cook for about 5 minutes.
- Rinse prawns and scallops and add to above mixture and sauté for a few minutes.
- Add the tomato juice, the rest of the meat, cayenne pepper, tabasco, thyme, bay leaves and salt and pepper. Rinse the black beans, add to mixture and simmer for about half an hour.
- Once the rice has finished cooking remove plastic and tinfoil and fluff with a fork. Combine the rice with the above mixture and mix thoroughly. Add salsa, lime juice and cilantro and adjust seasonings to taste.
- Serve with Jalapeno and Cheddar Cornbread.

Indonesian Peanut Butter Curry

A delightful blend of red curry, coconut milk, peanut butter, lemon grass and Sambal Oelek, an Indonesian blend of chilies.

12 Servings	32 Servings	60 Servings	Ingredients
3 Tbsp	8 Tbsp	1 cup	Oil
3 Tbsp	8 Tbsp	15 Tbsp	Minced Garlic
3 tsp	3 Tbsp	7 Tbsp	Minced Ginger
3-4 stalks	6-7 stalks	8-10 stalks	Lemon Grass
2	4	8	Diced Onions
3	8	15	Red Bell Pepper
2 348 ml cans	4 348 ml cans	8 348 ml cans	Chick peas
12	32	60	Chicken Breasts
1 Tbsp	3 Tbsp	5 Tbsp	Lemon Juice
3 Tbsp	1/2 cup	1 cup	Soya Sauce
1 Tbsp	3 Tbsp	5 Tbsp	Red Curry Paste
1 tsp	1 Tbsp	3 Tbsp	Sambal Oelek
1 Tbsp	2 Tbsp	3 Tbsp	Red Wine Vinegar
1 Tbsp	3 Tbsp	5 Tbsp	Cumin
1 cup	3 cups	5 cups	Peanut Butter
1 Tbsp	3 Tbsp	5 Tbsp	Honey
1 tsp	1 Tbsp	2 Tbsp	Sea Salt (or to taste)
1 tsp	1 Tbsp	2 Tbsp	Cracked Pepper (or to taste)
2 - 540ml cans	5 - 540 ml cans	8 - 540 ml cans	Coconut Milk

Directions:

- Dice chicken into medium-sized pieces and sauté in oil in a large rondeau or stock pot until browned on the outside.
- Peel and cut the onions in half and dice. Peel and mince garlic and ginger.
- Add onions, garlic and ginger to chicken and sauté until the onions are cooked.

- Wash and dice red pepper. Prepare lemon grass by cutting the top half off and discarding. Slice lemon grass in half and remove outer layers and discard. Cut the pieces of lemon grass in half again.
- Add red curry paste, lemon grass, soya sauce, sambal oelek, red peppers, red wine vinegar, cumin and peanut butter. Scoop the coconut milk off of the top of the coconut water and add to simmering ingredients. Drain and rinse chick peas and add to above ingredients. Add salt, pepper and honey to taste. Simmer until the flavors merge, then add the remainder of the coconut water and adjust seasoning to taste.
- Serve with rice and sautéed sambal oelek green beans.

Vegetarian Chick Pea Curry

There are many different types of curry available on the market today. For this dish I recommend a mild curry paste, especially when serving larger crowds as not everyone can tolerate the same level of heat.

12 Servings	32 Servings	60 Servings	Ingredients
2 Tbsp	4 Tbsp	6 Tbsp	Clarified Ghee, Coconut or Peanut Oil
3 Tbsp	8 Tbsp	12 Tbsp	Garlic
3 Tbsp	8 Tbsp	12 Tbsp	Ginger
3	5	8	Onions
3	8	15	Green or Red Bell Peppers
1 - 540 ml can	1 - 2.4 L can	2 - 2.4 L cans	Chick Peas
2-3 Tbsp	5-6 Tbsp	9-10 Tbsp	Mild Curry Paste
2 cups	8 cups	15 cups	Cream or Coconut Milk
1 Tbsp	3 Tbsp	6 Tbsp	Cumin
1 tsp	2 tsp	1 Tbsp	Toasted Cumin Seeds
1 Tbsp	3 Tbsp	5 Tbsp	Cane Sugar or Honey
1 Tbsp	2 Tbsp	3 Tbsp	Lemon Juice
3 Tbsp	1/2 cup	1 cup	Garam Masala
1/2 Tbsp	1 Tbsp	2 Tbsp	Sea Salt (or to taste)
3 Tbsp	8 Tbsp	15 Tbsp	Tomato Paste
1 Tbsp	3 Tbsp	5 Tbsp	Fresh Cilantro or Coriander
1 Tbsp	3 Tbsp	5 Tbsp	Grated Coconut

Directions:

- Peel and mince garlic and ginger. Peel onions and dice into medium-sized pieces. Wash and slice peppers in half, remove membrane and dice into medium-sized pieces.
- In a large stock pot, heat coconut oil or peanut oil and sauté onions, garlic and ginger. Add garam masala, cumin, curry paste, sugar and lemon juice to

garlic, ginger and onions. Toast cumin seeds in a frying pan over medium heat and add to above ingredients.

- Add diced red peppers and stir.
- Rinse and drain chick peas and add to mixture, stirring well so the chick peas are coated with curry mixture.
- Add cream or coconut milk and tomato paste and simmer until flavors merge. Add salt and pepper to taste.
- Top with minced cilantro or coriander and shredded coconut.
- Serve with chutney, rice pulao and naan bread.

Chicken Cacciatore

This recipe has loads of flavor and is a great way to use up leftover bacon. Depending on the size of the chicken thighs, I recommend two large thighs or 3-4 small chicken thighs per person.

12 Servings	32 Servings	60 Servings	Ingredients
34-36	90-96	180	Chicken Thighs
½ kg	1 kg	1 ½ kg	Cooked Diced Bacon
1	3	5	Zucchini
2 - 540 ml cans	1 - 2.4 L can	2 - 2.4 L cans	Tomato Sauce
1 156 ml can	2 156 ml cans	3 156 ml cans	Tomato Paste
2 - 250 ml cans	2 - 540 ml cans	1 2.4 L can	Diced Tomatoes
3 Tbsp	5 Tbsp	8 Tbsp	Olive Oil
2	4	8	Onion
3 Tbsp	8 Tbsp	12 Tbsp	Garlic
3 Tbsp	8 Tbsp	15 Tbsp	Basil
1 tsp	1 Tbsp	2 Tbsp	Celery Seed
1 Tbsp	3 Tbsp	5 Tbsp	Oregano
1 Tbsp	3 Tbsp	5 Tbsp	Thyme
2 tsp	3 tsp	4 tsp	Sea Salt (or to taste)
2 tsp	3 tsp	4 tsp	Pepper (or to taste)
5 cups	15 cups	24 cups	Chicken Broth
2	4	6	Bay Leaves
1 Tbsp	3 Tbsp	5 Tbsp	Sugar
¼ cup	¾ cups	1 ½ cups	Balsamic or Red Wine Vinegar or Red Wine
1 Tbsp	3 Tbsp	5 Tbsp	Lemon Juice
1 cup	3 cups	5 cups	Parmesan

Directions:

- In a large rondeau, heat oil over medium low heat and sauté chicken thighs in oil until browned. Once browned, remove from pan.

- Peel and remove onions and garlic and dice finely. Add to rondeau and sauté in the chicken juices until onions are translucent.
- Deglaze the pan by adding the balsamic, red wine vinegar or red wine. Add chicken broth and reduce until all the chicken pieces have loosened from the bottom of the pan.
- Add tomato sauce, tomato paste, basil, salt and pepper, oregano, thyme, bay leaves, celery seed, lemon juice, parmesan and sugar.
- Add chicken back to the sauce, as well as the diced bacon.
- Shred zucchini, add to sauce and simmer until the flavors merge.
- Serve over egg noodles or brown rice with roasted veggies on the side.

Thai Green Chicken Curry

A few years ago, I took a Thai cooking course in Chang Mai at a place called the Libra House where we learned to cook delicious dishes ranging from Pad Thai to traditional sticky rice and, of course, green curry. The following recipe is an adapted version of the Libra House recipe.

When cooking with curry, taste it as you go and add a bit at a time because you can't take the curry paste out, but you can always add more.

12 Servings	32 Servings	60 Servings	Ingredients
3 Tbsp	5 Tbsp	8 Tbsp	Coconut Oil
3	8	15	Onions
6 cloves	8 cloves	15 cloves	Garlic
6 Tbsp	16 Tbsp	30 Tbsp	Ginger
3	8	15	Red Bell Peppers
3	8	15	Carrots
1 ½ cups	4 cups	7 cups	Green Peas
2 - 240 ml cans	2 - 540 ml cans	4 - 540ml cans	Bamboo Shoots
18	48	90	Boneless/Skinless Chicken Thighs or Breasts
2 Tbsp	4-5 Tbsp	7-8 Tbsp	Green Curry Paste
4 240 ml cans	12 240 ml cans	18 240 ml cans	Coconut Milk
1 ½ Tbsp	5 Tbsp	8 Tbsp	Fish Sauce
5-6	8-10	14-15	Crushed Kaffir Lime Leaves
5-6 pieces	10-12 pieces	15-17 pieces	Lemon Grass
1 Tbsp	3 Tbsp	5 Tbsp	Cane Sugar
3 Tbsp	8 Tbsp	15 Tbsp	Fresh Cilantro or Basil
2	5	8	Limes
1 Tsp	1 Tbsp	2 Tbsp	Sea Salt (or to taste)

Directions:

- Dice chicken into chunks and sauté in coconut oil over medium heat in a large stock pot until almost cooked.

- Peel and dice onions into medium-sized pieces and add to chicken.
- Peel garlic and ginger, mince finely and add to the above.
- Peel carrots and julienne, add to chicken. Slice peppers in half; remove the membranes and dice, set aside.
- Chop the lemon grass from the middle of the stalk and discard the top. Then, slice in half lengthwise and cut into quarter pieces and discard the outer skin. You want the pieces to be big enough that you can pick them out from the rest of the dish. Lemon grass is not meant to be eaten.
- Add curry paste, lemon grass and fish sauce. Add the coconut milk solids from the top of the can, but not the coconut water. By adding only the coconut milk first, this will help release the flavors of the curry.
- Sauté until the oils from the curry paste have been released into the coconut milk.
- Then add coconut water, kaffirr lime leaves, fresh squeezed lime and cane sugar. Before adding the kaffir lime leaves release the flavors by rubbing the leaves in your palm and thumb.
- Add red pepper and green peas and simmer until flavors merge. Finish with a touch of salt to taste. Because the fish sauce is very salty, add salt in moderation.
- Top with finely diced basil or cilantro.
- Serve with brown basmati rice, jasmine rice or over linguine noodles.

Variation: Substitute Japanese squash, known as kombuchu for green peas. Peel and dice the squash into medium-sized pieces and roast in the oven over medium heat until soft and add to curry.

Stuffed Pork with Apricot & Ricotta Stuffing

Serve the stuffed pork loin with a side of apple sauce adding to the lovely blend of apricot, curry and ricotta.

12 Servings	32 Servings	60 Servings	Ingredients
1 large (6 lbs)	3 large (16 lbs)	6 large (30 lbs)	Pork Loin Roast
3 cups	8 cups	15 cups	Apricots
3 cups	8 cups	15 cups	Bread Crumbs
3 stalks	8 stalks	15 stalks	Celery
3	5	8	Onion
1 1/2 Tbsp	5 Tbsp	7 Tbsp	Yellow Curry
1 1/2 Tbsp	5 Tbsp	7 Tbsp	Thyme
1 Tbsp	2 Tbsp	3 Tbsp	Sea Salt
1 Tbsp	2 Tbsp	3 Tbsp	Pepper
4	6	8	Eggs
3 Tbsp	5 Tbsp	8 Tbsp	Butter
1 cup	2 cups	3 cups	Cream
3 cups	8 cups	15 cups	Ricotta

*Butcher's twine (approximately one 48 cm piece of twine for each loin)

Directions:

- Peel and slice onion in half and dice into small pieces. Wash and dice celery into small pieces.
- In a large pan, melt butter and sauté celery and onion in butter until soft. Add bread crumbs, set aside and let cool.
- Chop apricots in a food processor and add to bread crumbs.
- In large bowl combine bread crumb mixture, ricotta, eggs, cream, salt, thyme, yellow curry, pepper, onions and celery.
- Slice open pork loin horizontally in the middle and lay flat. Spoon mixture into center of loin. Fold half the loin over the other half and at one end of the loin wrap the twine around, making a knot with the shorter end. Wrap the rest of the twine around the rest of the loin until you reach the end, tie another knot and cut any excess twine away.

- Coat outside of loin with oil, thyme, salt and pepper. Bake slowly at 325°F for a couple of hours.
- Serve with apple sauce, mashed potatoes, green peas, roasted carrots and side green salad.

Vegetarian Shepherd's Pie

A savoury soul food dish…

12 Servings	32 Servings	60 Servings	Ingredients
24	64	120	Red Potatoes
3 Tbsp	8 Tbsp	15 Tbsp	Sour cream
3 Tbsp	5 Tbsp	8 Tbsp	Garlic
3 Tbsp	8 Tbsp	15 Tbsp	Milk
2 Tbsp	5Tbsp	8 Tbsp	Butter
1 tsp	1 Tbsp	2 Tbsp	Sea Salt (or to taste)
1 tsp	1 Tbsp	2 Tbsp	Pepper

Filling:

12 Servings	32 Servings	60 Servings	Ingredients
5	16	30	Carrots
5 stalks	16 stalks	30 stalks	Celery
6	16	30	Parsnips
3	8	15	Sweet Potatoes or Yams
3	8	15	Onions
1 bulb	3 bulbs	6 bulbs	Fresh Fennel
1 ½ cups	4 cups	7 cups	Peas
2 - 250 ml cans	3 - 250 ml cans	4 - 250 ml cans	Tomato Paste
1 cup	5 cups	9 cups	Tomato Juice
1 Tbsp	4 Tbsp	7 Tbsp	Cumin
1 Tbsp	3 Tbsp	5 Tbsp	Vegetarian Stock
2 tsp	1 Tbsp	2 Tbsp	Sea Salt (or to taste)
2 tsp	1 Tbsp	2 Tbsp	Pepper (or to taste)
2 tsp	2 Tbsp	5 Tbsp	Thyme
2 tsp	2 Tbsp	5 Tbsp	Rosemary
1 Tbsp	2 Tbsp	4 Tbsp	Turmeric
2 Tbsp	3 Tbsp	4 Tbsp	Olive Oil

Directions:

- Wash and scrub any spots off of the potatoes. Dice into quarters and place in a large pot with cold water and a sprinkle of salt. Bring to a boil. Drain, being sure to reserve a bit of the water, and place potatoes back into pot. Add salt, pepper, minced garlic, butter, cream and mash until smooth. You can also blend with a hand blender so the potatoes form a smooth, creamy consistency. Set aside.
- Peel and dice sweet potatoes or yams, parsnips, carrots, and onion into medium-sized pieces. Dice celery into medium-sized pieces as well.
- Cut the top off the fennel bulb and discard the top but keep the anise herbs. The herb located at the top of the bulb is called anise and can be used in the dish. Remove the anise herb and mince finely. Slice fennel in half, remove the outer layer and julienne fennel into long skinny pieces.
- Heat oil in a large stock pot and sauté veggies in a pan starting with the onions, then adding the root veggies and finally the celery and fennel. Add peas, tomato paste, cumin, nutmeg, celery seed, thyme, rosemary, turmeric, veggie stock, salt and pepper. Add tomato juice to the mixture to help thin out the tomato paste. Adjust seasonings to taste.
- Spoon veggie mixture into a greased casserole dish, top off with potatoes and sprinkle with paprika.
- Bake at 375°F until top is golden brown.
- Serve with Green Onion Biscuits and Miso Gravy.

Beef Stroganoff

This dish is creamy and delicious. Make sure to have lots of mushrooms on hand as they will shrink considerably as the dish cooks.

12 Servings	32 Servings	60 Servings	Ingredients
3	8	15	Onions
1 ½ kg	4 kg	12 kg	Brown Mushrooms
3 kg	8 kg	15 kg	Stewing Beef
3 cups	8 cups	15 cups	Flour
1/4 cup	¾ cup	11/4 cup	Red Wine or Red Wine Vinegar
1 cup	3 cup	5 cups	Beef Stock
3 cups	8 cups	15 cups	Water
3 Tbsp	8 Tbsp	12 Tbsp	Dijon Mustard
3 cups	8 cups	12 cups	Sour Cream
3 Tbsp	8 Tbsp	12 Tbsp	Tahini
3 Tbsp	8 Tbsp	12 Tbsp	Garlic
1tsp each	1 Tbsp each	1 1/2 Tbsp each	Salt and Pepper (or to taste)
4 Tbsp	8 Tbsp	12 Tbsp	Fresh Dill
2	3	4	Bay Leaves

Directions:

- Measure flour into a large bowl.
- Cut beef into bite-sized chunks and dredge lightly in flour. Heat oil in a large pan or rondeau and sauté beef lightly until brown on both sides. Remove beef and set aside.
- Peel onions and chop into medium-sized pieces. Sauté in the pan with beef fat until almost translucent. Deglaze the pan with the red wine or red wine vinegar and reduce. Slice mushrooms and garlic; add to rondeau and cook until onions are carmelized.
- Add beef stock, Dijon mustard, sour cream, tahini and bay leaves.
- Mince fresh dill and add to above ingredients.
- Simmer for 10 minutes; add beef and simmer for two minutes or until beef has achieved desired texture. Add salt and pepper.
- Serve over medium broad egg noodles with green beans as a side.

Vegetarian Moroccan Stew

A savory blend of spices that adds a hint of warmth to any cold day…

12 Servings	32 Servings	60 Servings	Ingredients
8 Tbsp	12 Tbsp	15 Tbsp	Oil
2	4	8	Onions
6-7 cloves	8-9 cloves	12-15 cloves	Garlic
¼ cup	½ cup	¾ cups	Vegetable Stock
3 cups	5 cups	8 cups	Tomato Juice
3 cups	8 cups	12 cups	Butternut Squash
2	4	6	Yams
5	8	15	Bakers Potato
8 stalks	1 head	2 heads	Celery
2	5	8	Parsnips
1	3	5	Zucchini
3	5	8	Carrots
2 - 250 ml	1 - 2.4 L cans	2 - 2.4 L cans	Diced Tomatoes
½ - 6oz can	1 - 6oz can	2 - 6oz cans	Tomato Paste
1 - 250 ml cans	2 - 250 ml cans	1 - 2.4 L can	Chick Peas
3 Tbsp	9 Tbsp	15 Tbsp	Cumin
1 Tbsp	3 Tbsp	5 Tbsp	Chili Powder
3 Tbsp	5 Tbsp	8 Tbsp	Cardamom
1 Tbsp	3 Tbsp	5 Tbsp	Cinnamon
1 tsp	1 Tbsp	1 ½ Tbsp	Cloves
1 tsp	1 Tbsp	1 ½ Tbsp	Nutmeg
1 Tbsp	3 Tbsp	5 Tbsp	Coriander

Directions:

- In a large stock pot, heat oil over medium low heat. Peel and dice garlic and onions, add to oil and begin sautéing.
- Peel yams, squash, parsnips and carrots. Dice into small cubes and add to sautéing onions and garlic. Dice potatoes into small, quarter-sized pieces. Add quartered potatoes, cumin, chili powder, cardamom, cinnamon, cloves,

nutmeg and coriander to sautéing vegetables and continue sautéing for a couple of minutes longer.

- Slice celery into half-inch pieces. Dice the celery rib into small pieces. Wash and dice zucchini, then add celery and zucchini to above vegetables.
- Add tomato paste, tomato juice and stock and cook vegetables until soft.
- Drain chick peas and add to veggies once some of the liquid has been absorbed by the vegetables.
- Add salt and pepper to taste and adjust other seasonings, also to taste. Let flavors merge, then serve over brown rice.

Butter Chicken

Also known as Makhan Murg, this East Indian Dish is creamy with a hint of spice and boasts many compliments.

12 Servings	32 Servings	60 Servings	Ingredients
5 Tbsp	½ cup	1 cup	Clarified Butter or Coconut Oil
9	24	45	Chicken Breasts (large)
3	5	8	Onions
7-8 cloves	12-15 cloves	21-24 cloves	Garlic
6 Tbsp	½ cup	1 cup	Minced Fresh Ginger
6 Tbsp	1 cup	1 ½ cups	Garam Masala
1 tsp	1 Tbsp	2 Tbsp	Red Chili Powder or Cayenne Powder
1 Tbsp	3 Tbsp	5 Tbsp	Cumin
1 Tbsp	1 ½ Tbsp	2 Tbsp	Sea Salt (or to taste}
2 - 250 ml cans	1 - 2.4 L cans	2 - 2.4 L cans	Diced Tomatoes plus juice
1 156 ml cans	2 156 ml cans	3 156 ml cans	Tomato Paste
6 Tbsp	½ cup	1 cup	Tandoori Paste
2 L	8 L	15 L	Heavy Whipping Cream
¾ cup	2 cups	4 cups	Plain Yogurt
3 Tbsp	5 Tbsp	8 Tbsp	Honey
2 Tbsp	5 Tbsp	½ Cup	Kasuri Methi Leaves or Fresh Coriander

Directions:

- Dice chicken into medium-sized pieces.
- Heat clarified butter in a large stock pot, add diced chicken and begin sautéing. Peel and mince onion, garlic and ginger.
- Add onion, garlic, ginger, and garam masala and sauté with chicken until golden brown.

- Add tandoori paste and tomato paste and sauté until the oils from the tandoori paste are released. Then add diced tomatoes and juice.
- Add whipping cream, yogurt, honey, salt and pepper and let simmer until chicken is tender.
- Garnish with minced kasuri methi leaves or coriander.
- Serve with naan, rice pulao, red lentil curry or curried chick peas and vegetables.

Creamy Paneer Curry with Green Peas

An excellent source of protein, paneer is a soft curd cheese made from curdled milk and lemon juice and is available in the frozen section in most large grocery stores.

12 Servings	32 Servings	60 Servings	Ingredients
3 Tbsp	8 Tbsp	1 cup	Clarified Butter (Ghee*) or Coconut Oil
6 cups	16 cups	30 cups	Paneer*
2	4	6	Onions
6-7 cloves	12-13 cloves	18-20 cloves	Garlic
3 Tbsp	8 Tbsp	1 cup	Minced Ginger
6 Tbsp	1 cup	1 ½ cups	Garam Masala
2 Tbsp	5 Tbsp	8 Tbsp	Pataks Mild Curry Paste
1 tsp	1 Tbsp	1 ½ Tbsp	Chilli Powder or Cayenne Powder
1 Tbsp	5 Tbsp	8 Tbsp	Cumin
2 tsp	1 Tbsp	1 ½ Tbsp	Sea Salt (or to taste)
2 - 250 ml cans	1 - 2.4 L can	2 - 2.4 L cans	Diced Tomatoes plus juice
1 156 ml can	2 156 ml cans	3 156 ml cans	Tomato Paste
3 cups	8 cups	15 cups	Green Peas
2 L	8 L	15 L	Heavy Whipping Cream
¾ cup	2 cups	4 cups	Plain Yogurt
3 Tbsp	5 Tbsp	8 Tbsp	Honey
3 Tbsp	8 Tbsp	1 cup	Kasuri Methi* Leaves or Fresh Coriander

You may find foods like paneer, ghee and kasuri methi in the specialty aisle of your supermarket, or hunt for an Asian foods market in your area.

Directions:

- Sauté paneer (Indian cheese curds) in clarified butter until golden brown and set aside.

- Peel and dice onions into medium-sized pieces.
- Mince garlic and ginger.
- Over medium heat, sauté onions in ghee until almost cooked. Add ginger, garlic, curry paste, garam masala, cumin and cayenne pepper.
- Sauté the onions and garlic until the oils from the curry are released. You will be able to see oils separate from the rest of the ingredients.
- Add diced tomatoes and juice, cream, yoghurt and tomato paste.
- Add paneer, green peas, honey, salt and minced kasuri methi leaves or fresh coriander.
- Let the flavors merge and adjust seasonings accordingly. Serve with basmati rice and naan bread.

Roast Chicken with Rice Stuffing

Nothing beats this classic recipe. I like to add sliced lemon slices to the chickens for a savory touch.

12 Servings	32 Servings	60 Servings	Ingredients
6 kg	16 kg	30 kg	Whole Roasting Chicken
1 ½ cups	3 cups	4 cups	Butter
12	18	24	Garlic Cloves
1 Tbsp	3 Tbsp	5 Tbsp	Ground Thyme
1 Tbsp	3 Tbsp	5 Tbsp	Sage
1 Tbsp	3 Tbsp	5 Tbsp	Cumin
1 Tbsp	3 Tbsp	5 Tbsp	Marjoram
2 Tsp	2 Tbsp	3 Tbsp	Nutmeg
1 Tbsp	3 Tbsp	5 Tbsp	Chopped Fresh Rosemary
1 Tbsp	3 Tbsp	5 Tbsp	Mrs. Dash
2	6	12	Lemons
5 Tbsp	8 Tbsp	15 Tbsp	Olive Oil

Stuffing:

12 Servings	32 Servings	60 Servings	Ingredients
6 cups	16 cups	30 cups	Cooked Brown Rice
1 ½ cups	3 cups	7 ½ cups	Diced Celery
1 ½ cups	3 cups	7 ½ cups	Diced Onion
1 ½ cups	3 cups	7 ½ cups	Diced Brown Mushrooms
8 cloves	12 cloves	15 cloves	Garlic (minced)
1 cup	3 cups	5 cups	Chicken Broth
1 ½ cups	2 cups	4 cups	Chopped Sundried Tomatoes
1 ½ cups	2 cups	4 cups	Chopped Fresh Parsley

Directions:

- Cook brown rice and set aside.
- Dice carrots, celery, onions, and mushrooms and mince garlic.
- Sauté above veggies in either oil or butter. Add chicken broth to mixture, then sauté until lightly cooked. Set aside and let cool.
- Mix together thyme, sage, marjoram, rosemary and Mrs. Dash. Instead of buying these spices separately, you could buy a ready-made poultry seasoning. Chop both the sundried tomatoes and parsley.
- Once sautéed veggies and rice have cooled, mix together. Add sundried tomatoes, parsley and seasoning with half the poultry seasonings (thyme, sage, marjoram, nutmeg, cumin, ground rosemary).
- Preheat oven to 450°F. Now it's time to clean the bird! Remove insides (gizzards, liver, and neck) and place in a pot. Rinse the bird inside and out and pat dry with paper towel.
- Slit the bird just above the drumstick. Some birds may already have an opening here on both sides and some may not. Rub butter all over the bird both inside and outside the cavity and in the slits above the drumsticks. Cut a piece of garlic in half and rub over bird. Place garlic pieces inside of the bird or in the slits on the side. Salt and pepper the bird both inside and out.
- Stuff the bird with the rice mixture, making sure to fill every cavity and if you want you can even add stuffing to the sides above the drumstick if there is a space for you to do so.
- Close the front of bird with butcher's twine, metal pins or bamboo skewers soaked in water.
- Sprinkle the remainder if the poultry seasoning, minced rosemary and Mrs. Dash on the bird and drizzle with olive oil. Add a bit of water just to cover the bottom of the pan to prevent burning. Place a piece of folded foil over the areas where the stuffing is exposed to prevent it from burning.
- Place bird in a preheated oven at 425°F for 15 minutes, then turn down the oven temperature from 425 to 350°F and cook until the bird reaches 165°F internally. (This will take about 30 minutes per pound, or if non-stuffed reduce by 10 minutes for each pound). Let rest for 15-20 minutes before carving.
- Serve with roasted veggies.

Baked Salmon with Strawberries, Mangoes & Balsamic Reduction

The blend of fresh fruit and balsamic add refreshing taste to baked salmon.

12 Servings	32 Servings	60 Servings	Ingredients
3	8	15	Large Salmon
3 Cups	8 Cups	15 Cups	Fresh Strawberries
3 Cups	8 Cups	15 Cups	Fresh Mangoes
1 ½ Cup	4 Cups	7 ½ Cups	Balsamic reduction
3 Tbsp	8 Tbsp	15 Tbsp	Butter
1 Tbsp	2 Tbsp	3 Tbsp	Sea Salt
1 Tbsp	2 Tbsp	3 Tbsp	Pepper
1 Tbsp	2 Tbsp	3 Tbsp	Lemon Juice

Directions:

- Preheat oven to 350 °F.
- Wash and thinly slice strawberries. Peel mangoes and dice into small pieces. Prepare balsamic reduction according to directions on pg. () before hand and set aside. Note: As the balsamic reduction cools it will thicken so you may have to heat slightly before drizzling over the Salmon.
- Rinse salmon and pat dry. Tray out parchment paper onto a large hotel tray. Place salmon onto tray and sprinkle with salt and pepper, a tablespoon of butter for each salmon piece and a squeeze lemon. Bake salmon for 25 minutes or until cooked all the way through.
- Place strawberries and mangoes over the salmon and drizzle with balsamic.
- Serve immediately with roasted asparagus and rice pilaf.

Panko Breaded Halibut with Tarragon Cream Sauce

Heavenly and rich, this extremely easy dish to prepare will leave you wanting more.

12 Servings	32 Servings	60 Servings	Ingredients
12	32	60	Halibut Pieces
6 cups	15 cups	30 cups	Panko Flakes
6 cups	15 cups	30 cups	Flour
6	15	30	Eggs
1 ½ cups	4 cups	7 cups	Milk
3 cups	8 cups	15 cups	Sour Cream
5 cups	12 cups	24 cups	Heavy Whipping Cream
40 g	60 g	80 g	Onion Soup Mix
3 cups	8 cups	15 cups	Grated Parmesan
1 Tbsp	3 Tbsp	5 Tbsp	Fresh Tarragon
½ Tbsp	1 Tbsp	2 Tbsp	Sea Salt
½ Tbsp	1 Tbsp	2 Tbsp	Pepper

Panko is a Japanese breadcrumb that has flaky, airier texture resulting in a crispier coating.

Directions:

- Rinse and pat halibut dry and set aside.
- In a large bowl, combine sour cream, heavy whipping cream, onion soup mix, grated parmesan and minced tarragon.
- Combine panko flakes, salt and pepper. Combine eggs and milk and whisk together.
- Dredge halibut in flour, the dip into egg mixture and coat both sides with the panko mixture and place breaded halibut pieces into a 4 inch greased hotel pan. Pour sour cream mixture over the halibut pieces and cook in a preheated oven at 350°F for 40 minutes or until halibut is cooked all the way through.

Camp Sized Pizzas

When making pizza for large crowds I find that it is easiest to use medium to large cookie sheets. You might have to stretch the dough a couple of times to get it to fit properly. *Quick Tip: You can pre-make the dough and then cover it with plastic wrap and place it in the freezer until needed.*

Margherita Pizza

Use fresh ripe tomatoes with minced garlic to make a delicious vegetarian entrée.

12 Servings	32 Servings	60 Servings	Ingredients
3	8	15	Large Crusts
3 cups	8 cups	15 cups	Pizza Sauce
3 Tbsp	8 Tbsp	15 Tbsp	Crushed Garlic
6	16	30	Sliced Tomatoes
4 cups	12 cups	22 cups	Pizza Mozzarella

Directions:

- Prepare pizza dough and sauce according to the recipes in this book.
- Slice tomatoes into rounds.
- Spoon pizza sauce onto unbaked pizza crust and layer with crushed garlic, then tomatoes and finally a nice thick layer of mozza.
- Bake at 400°F for 30 minutes or until crust is browned and cheese is melted and browned on top.

BBQ Chicken & Chorizo with Caramelized Onions

When making pizza, I always have my toppings prepared in advance so it is easier and faster to assemble.

12 Servings	32 Servings	60 Servings	Ingredients
3 pieces	12 pieces	24 pieces	Cooked Chicken Breasts
3 cups	8 cups	15 cups	Cooked Chorizo
1 cup	3 cups	5 cups	BBQ Sauce
3	5	8	Red Pepper
1	3	5	Red Onions
3 Tbsp	5 Tbsp	8 Tbsp	Butter or oil
3	8	15	Large Crusts
3 Cups	8 Cups	15 Cups	Pizza Sauce
4 Cups	12 Cups	22 Cups	Pizza Mozzarella

Directions:

- Prepare pizza dough and sauce according to the recipes in this book.
- Tray out chicken and chorizo (on separate pans) with parchment placed on the bottom. Sprinkle chicken with salt and pepper.
- Cook Chicken and Chorizo in the oven at 350 until done. Remove from oven and let cool. Cube chicken into small pieces and toss in BBQ sauce. Any zesty BBQ sauce will do. Slice chorizo into thin coins.
- Peel and slice onions into long strips. Caramelize by cooking a large frying pan with butter or oil for about 45 minutes or until the onions are nice and browned. Set aside and let cool.
- Dice red pepper into small pieces and set aside.
- Shred pizza mozzarella and set aside.
- Spoon pizza sauce onto unbaked pizza crust and layer with onions, red pepper, chorizo and diced chicken and finally a nice thick layer of mozza.
- Bake at 400 for 30 minutes or until crust is browned and cheese is melted and browned on top

Other Pizza Toppings:

- Sliced Black Olives
- Artichokes
- Feta
- Real Bacon Bits
- Pesto
- Mushrooms
- Sundried Tomatoes
- Pineapple
- Ham
- Grilled Zucchini
- Grilled Eggplant
- Smoked Tofu

Baked Rigatoni with Chorizo

A delicious hearty meal with a little kick from the chorizo, a spicy Italian sausage.

12 Servings	32 Servings	60 Servings	Ingredients
6 Cups	15 Cups	30 Cups	Penne
10 Cups	28 Cups	50 Cups	Water
10 Cups	28 Cups	58 Cups	Basic Meat Sauce
3 sausages	8 sausages	15 sausages	Chorizo
3 Cups	7 Cups	12 Cups	Grated Marble Cheese
1 Cup	3 Cups	5 Cups	Parmesan
¼ Cup	½ Cup	¾ Cup	Dried Parsley

Directions:

- Prepare basic meat sauce according to the recipe in this book.
- Bake chorizo according to the directions on the package. Set aside and let cool. Slice chorizo into small ¼ inch thick coins.
- Bring water to a boil and salt. Add penne noodles and boil for about 20 minutes, or until the edges of the noodle have turned a white in comparison to the rest of the noodle. You want the noodles to be al dente, as they will continue to cook in the sauce as it bakes in the oven. Drain noodles and set aside.
- Grate marble cheese and set aside.
- Divide chorizo and sauce between the hotel pans.
- Layer cheese on top of pasta and sprinkle with parmesan and dried parsley.
- Cover with a hotel lid or plastic wrap followed by a layer of tinfoil. Bake for 45 minutes or until cheese has melted. Remove cover and let cheese brown slightly. Remove from oven and let cool slightly.

DESSERTS, SQUARES & BAKED GOODS

Apple Crisp

A delicious and simple dessert that pairs nicely with ice cream on a hot day.

12 Servings	32 Servings	60 Servings	Ingredients
2 kg	6 kg	12 kg	Granny Smith Apples (fresh or frozen)
1 Tbsp	2 Tbsp	3 Tbsp	Vanilla
1 Tbsp	2 Tbsp	3 Tbsp	Lemon Juice
½ cup	1 cup	1 ½ cups	Maple Syrup (or to taste)
1 Tbsp	4 Tbsp	8 Tbsp	Cinnamon
¾ cup	1 cup	1 ½ cups	Butter or Margarine

Topping:

12 Servings	32 Servings	60 Servings	Ingredients
9 cups	24 cups	45 cups	Rolled Oats
1 ½ cups	3 cups	4 cups	Whole Wheat Flour
1 ½ cups	3 cups	5 cups	Butter or non-hydrogenated Margarine
1 Tbsp	3 Tbsp	5 Tbsp	Vanilla
1 cup	2 cups	3 cups	Brown Sugar
1 Tbsp	4 Tbsp	8 Tbsp	Cinnamon (or to taste)
1 tsp	1 Tbsp	1 1/2 Tbsp	Salt
¾ cup	1 ½ cups	2 cups	Slivered Almonds

Directions:

- Peel, core and slice apples into ¼ inch pieces. Sprinkle lemon juice over peeled apples to prevent them from browning.
- In a large bowl, mix apples with vanilla, maple syrup and cinnamon. Cut butter or margarine into chunks and add to the apple mixture.
- Mix oats with flour, hard butter, vanilla, brown sugar and cinnamon.
- Sprinkle 1/4 of oat mixture on the bottom of a glass dish. Layer apples on top and finish with the remainder of the oat mixture.

- Sprinkle with slivered almonds and bake in a preheated oven at 350°F for 45 minutes to an hour.
- Serve with ice cream.

Variation: Drizzle apple crisp with caramel sauce after baking.

Berry Crisp

Use frozen mixed berries or straight-up blueberries for this scrumptious favorite.

12 Servings	32 Servings	60 Servings	Ingredients
12 cups	32 cups	60 cups	Frozen Berries
1 Tbsp	3 Tbsp	5 Tbsp	Vanilla
1/2 cup	1 cup	1 ½ cups	Brown Sugar or Honey
1 Tbsp	4 Tbsp	8 Tbsp	Cinnamon
¾ cup	1 cup	1 ½ cups	Butter or non-hydrogenated Margarine

Topping:

9 cups	24 cups	45 cups	Rolled Oats
1 ½ cups	3 cups	4 cups	Whole Wheat Flour
1 ½ cups	3 cups	5 cups	Butter or Margarine
1 Tbsp	3 Tbsp	5 Tbsp	Vanilla
1 cup	2 cups	3 cups	Brown Sugar
1 Tbsp	4 Tbsp	8 Tbsp	Cinnamon (or to taste)
1 ½ Tsp	1 Tbsp	1 ½ Tbsp	Salt
¾ cup	1 ½ cups	2 cups	Slivered Almonds

Directions:

- Place frozen mixed berries in a greased 2 inch deep hotel insert.
- Sprinkle with cinnamon, vanilla, brown sugar or honey and butter and toss together.
- Mix oats with flour, hard butter, vanilla, brown sugar and cinnamon.
- Sprinkle oat mixture on top of berries and sprinkle with slivered almonds.
- Bake in oven at 350°F for about 45 minutes to an hour.
- Serve with ice cream.

Blueberry and Cream Cheese Squares – Version I

This no-bake dessert is simple and delicious and is sure to wow! You can also substitute the blueberry pie filling for cherry or strawberry.

12 Servings	32 Servings	60 Servings	Ingredients
Crust:			
6 cups	16 cups	30 cups	Graham Cracker Crumbs
1 ½ cups	4 cups	7 cups	Melted Butter
2 Tbsp	4 Tbsp	8 Tbsp	Brown Sugar
2 – 300 g packages	½ kg	1 kg	Cream Cheese
¾ cup	2 cups	4 cups	Milk
6 Tbsp	1 cup	2 cups	Confectioners' Sugar
Filling:			
3 cups	8 cups	15 cups	Heavy Whipping Cream
9 Tbsp	1 ½ cups	2 cups	Cane Sugar
2 Tbsp	6 Tbsp	10 Tbsp	Vanilla
Topping:			
2 - 540 ml cans	6 - 540 ml cans	8 - 540 ml cans	Blueberry or Cherry Pie Filling

Directions:

- In a medium-sized sauce pan melt butter or non-hydrogenated margarine over medium heat.
- Mix graham crumbs, brown sugar and butter, set aside ¼ of mixture for topping, and press the rest of the crumbs into the bottom of a 2 inch deep hotel insert. Chill in fridge for at least an hour.
- In a large mixing bowl using either a hand held mixer or a stand blender, beat cream cheese, confectioners' sugar, milk and ½ of the vanilla until smooth.

Spread evenly over the graham crumbs. Spread pie filing evenly over the cream cheese layer and chill.

- In a chilled bowl, whip the heavy cream, sugar and vanilla until stiff and spread over top of blueberry mixture.
- Sprinkle the top with the remaining graham crumbs and chill until served.
- If you are unable to find pre-ground graham cracker crumbs, buy whole graham crackers and blend in food processor into medium fine crumbs.

Blueberry and Cream Cheese Squares – Version 2

In this version, omit the real whipped cream and use instant whipped topping. I find the generic brand works the best in terms of time it takes to whip and the quality is just as good.

12 Servings	32 Servings	60 Servings	Ingredients
Crust:			
6 cups	16 cups	30 cups	Graham Cracker Crumbs
1 ½ cups	4 cups	7 cups	Melted Butter
2 Tbsp	4 Tbsp	8 Tbsp	Brown Sugar
Filling:			
2 – 300 g packages	½ kg	1 kg	Cream Cheese
¾ cup	2 cups	4 cups	Milk
2 - 80 g packages	4 - 80 g packages	6 - 80 g packages	Instant Whipped Topping
9 Tbsp	1 ½ cups	2 cups	Cane Sugar
2 Tbsp	6 Tbsp	10 Tbsp	Vanilla
Topping:			
2 - 540 ml cans	6 - 540 ml cans	8 - 540 ml cans	Blueberry or Cherry Pie Filling

Directions:

- Melt butter in a medium-sized sauce pan over medium heat.
- Mix graham crumbs, brown sugar and butter, set aside ¼ of mixture for topping, and press the rest of the crumbs into the bottom of a 2 inch deep hotel pan. Chill in fridge.
- Beat cream cheese, ½ of the vanilla, ½ of the instant whip and milk until smooth. Spread evenly over the graham crumbs. Spread pie filing evenly over the cream cheese layer and chill for a couple of hours.
- To prepare the instant whip, follow directions on the package. Once whipped, spread evenly over the cream cheese and pie filling layers.
- Sprinkle the top with the remaining graham crumbs and chill until served.

Layered Cream Cheese Dessert

A delightful blend of cream cheese and chocolate pudding is sure to please. Try topping with chocolate sprinkles.

12 Servings	32 Servings	60 Servings	Ingredients
4 cups	12 cups	22 cups	Oreo Cookie Crumbs
1 ½ cups	4 cups	7 cups	Butter
3 - 8oz packages	1 kg	1 ½ kg	Cream Cheese
3 Tsp	1 Tbsp	2 Tbsp	Vanilla
3 Tbsp	8 Tbsp	1 cup	Confectioners' Sugar
¾ cup	2 cups	3 ¾ cups	Milk
3 - 40g packages	6 - 40g packages	12 - 40 g packages	Powdered Instant Chocolate Pudding
1 L	1 ½ L	2 L	Whipping Cream
¾ cup	2 cups	3 ¾ cups	Sugar
1 Tbsp	2 Tbsp	3 Tbsp	Vanilla

Directions:

- In large heavy bottom pot, melt butter over medium low heat and mix Oreo cookie crumbs with the butter.
- Spread evenly over a pan and let cool.
- Use softened cream cheese and mix with vanilla, milk and confectioners' sugar and beat until light and fluffy.
- Spread evenly over the Oreo cookie crumbs.
- Follow directions of the instant chocolate pudding package and spread evenly over the cream cheese layer.
- Prepare whipped cream by pouring whipping cream into a chilled bowl. Add sugar and vanilla and whip until light and fluffy.
- Add evenly over the chocolate pudding mixture.
- Top with chocolate sprinkles. Set in fridge for at least 1 hour to allow for it to set.

Simple Baked Cheesecake

As the name suggests, a simple and easy dessert that will satisfy any sweet craving.

12 Servings	32 Servings	60 Servings	Ingredients
Crust:			
3 ¾ cups	10 cups	22 ½ cups	Graham Cracker Crumbs
1 cup	2 ¾ cups	5 cups	Melted Butter
6 Tbsp	1 cup	2 cups	Brown Sugar
Filling:			
300 g	1 kg	1 ½ kg	Cream Cheese
2 ¼ cup	6 cups	11 ¼ cups	Granulated Sugar
9	24	45	Eggs
¾ tsp	2 tsp	1 ½ Tbsp	Vanilla
1 Tbsp	3 Tbsp	5 Tbsp	Lemon Zest
3 cups	8 cups	15 cups	Sour Cream
¾ cup	2 cups	3 ¾ cups	Sugar
Topping:			
2 - 540 ml cans	5 - 540 ml cans	8 - 540 ml cans	Cherry or Blueberry Canned Filling

Directions:

- Preheat oven to 350°F.
- Take the cream cheese out of the fridge at bring to room temperature.
- Over medium low heat, melt butter in a heavy bottomed stock pot and remove from heat once melted. Add graham crumbs and sugar to the butter and mix. In a large 2 inch hotel pan, press graham crumb mixture into the pan and bake for 8-12 minutes and let cool.
- Meanwhile, in a large mixture beat softened cream cheese, sugar, eggs, vanilla and lemon zest together.

- Pour mixture over cooled crust and bake for 45 minutes or until the filling has set. Cracks will form on the top once it is has set.
- Combine sourcream and sugar.
- Remove from oven, place sour cream mixture over the cheesecake and bake for another 8-10 minutes.
- Remove from oven and let cool for 1 hour.
- Spread pie filling evenly over the cheesecake and chill.

Judy's Frozen Mousse Delight

This recipe I stumbled upon when I accidently left the dessert in the freezer and it turned into a frozen mouse that tastes just like ice cream cake but without the ice cream.

12 Servings	32 Servings	60 Servings	Ingredients
3 ¾ cups	10 cups	22 ½ cups	Graham Cracker
1 cup	2 ¾ cups	5 cups	Melted Butter
6 Tbsp	1 cup	2 cups	Brown Sugar
2 - 80 g packages	5-80 g packages	8-80 g packages	Chocolate Mousse
1-80 g package	3-80 g packages	5-80 g packages	Instant Whipped Topping
2 L	3 L	4 L	Milk

Directions:

- Prepare crust by melting butter over medium low heat and combining graham crumbs and brown sugar.
- Press into a 2 inch hotel pan and let set in fridge for 1 hour.
- Follow instructions on chocolate mousse package. Layer chocolate mousse over graham crumbs.
- Follow instructions on instant whipped topping. Layer on top of chocolate mousse.
- Sprinkle chocolate sprinkles evenly over whipped topping and place in freezer for 2 hours before serving.

Crisped Rice Squares

An old time classic… try adding goodies like gummy bears or toffee bits for a different twist.

12 servings	32 Servings	60 Servings	Ingredients
1 Tbsp	3 Tbsp	5 Tbsp	Vanilla
¼ Cup	1 Cup	2 Cups	Butter or non-hydrogenated margarine
1 package	3 packages	5 packages	Regular Marshmallows
6 Cups	18 Cups	36 cups	Crisped Rice Cereal

Directions:

- In a large stock pot, melt butter over medium low heat.
- Add marshmallows and melt while stirring constantly.
- Once marshmallows have melted add vanilla and remove from heat. Stir in the crisped rice until well coated. If using some of the options below, stir into the crisped rice right before you are finished mixing all the ingredients.
- Line a large hotel sheet with parchment paper and place aside a small bowl of water. To help prevent the crisped rice from sticking to your fingers, dip your hands in the water and removed crisped rice from the pot and place onto the hotel sheet. Push the crisped rice up against the edges and press down firmly.
- Let cool and cut into desired squares.

Optional:

- Gummy Bears
- Mixed Nuts
- Chocolate chips
- Caramel chips
- Toffee pieces

Chewy Toffee Almond Bars

Rich, chewy and full of toffee flavour… doesn't take much with this treat to satisfy your toffe cravings!

12 Servings	32 Servings	60 Servings	Ingredients
3 cups	8 cups	15 cups	Butter
1 ½ cups	4 cups	7 cups	Brown Sugar
6 cups	16 cups	30 cups	All – purpose Flour
5 ¼ cups	14 cups	26 cups	Toffee Bits
2 ¼ cups	6 cups	11 ¼ cups	Corn Syrup
3 cups	8 cups	15 cups	Sliced Almonds
2 ¼ cups	6 cups	11 ¼ cups	Sweetened Coconut Flakes

Directions:

- Preheat oven to 350°F.
- Lay parchment down on a large hotel sheet.
- Cream butter or non-hydrogenated margarine and sugar until fluffy.
- Gradually add flour, beating until well blended. Press dough evenly over pan.
- Bake for 15-20 minutes until edges are lightly browned.
- Meanwhile, combine 1 ¾ cup toffee bits and corn syrup in a medium sauce pan. Melt over medium heat, stirring constantly until toffee is melted.
- Stir in ½ cup of coconut and sliced almonds. Spread toffee mixture to within ¼ inch of edges of crust.
- Sprinkle remaining sliced almonds, toffee bits and coconut over toffee layer.
- Bake for 15 minutes or until bubbly.
- Cool and cut into bars into desired size.

Chocolate Peanut Butter Squares

A rich and delicious treat!

12 Servings	32 Servings	60 Servings	Ingredients
1 ½ cups	4 cups	7 cups	Margarine or Butter
2 ¼ cups	6 cups	11 ¼ cups	Smooth Peanut Butter
6 cups	16 cups	30 cups	Confectioners' Icing Sugar
1 ½ cups	4 cups	7 cups	Graham Cracker Crumbs
4 cups	12 cups	24 cups	Semi-Sweet Chocolate Chips
6 Tbsp	1 cup	1 ¼ cups	Hard Margarine or Butter

Directions:

- In a medium sauce pan over medium low heat, melt first amount of butter over low heat. Stir in peanut butter and blend until smooth.
- Remove from heat and add the icing sugar and graham crumbs.
- Line a baking sheet with parchment and pat peanut butter mixture into pan. Let cool in a freezer.
- Over medium low heat, melt second amount of butter in a medium saucepan, add chocolate and blend until smooth.
- Add chocolate layer to peanut butter layer and let cool. Cut into desired squares.

Chocolate Crunch Bars

To help prevent this sticky number from sticking to your hands have a bowl of cold water ready to dips your hands into.

12 Servings	32 Servings	60 Servings	Ingredients
1 ½ cups	4 cups	7 cups	Peanut Butter
1 ½ cups	4 cups	7 cups	Corn Syrup
1 ½ cups	4 cups	7 cups	Brown Sugar
9 cups	24 cups	45 cups	Crisped Rice or Corn Fakes
¾ cup	2 cups	4 cups	Peanuts
3 cups	8 cups	15 cups	Semi-Sweet Chocolate Chips
3 Tbsp	8 Tbsp	1 cup	Non-hydrogenated Margarine or Butter

Directions:

- Over medium heat, in a large heavy bottomed stock pot melt together corn syrup, peanut butter and brown sugar.
- Once heated, add the crisped rice or corn flakes and peanuts and mix together until the cereal is well coated.
- Using a large hotel cookie sheet, spread parchment over the cookie sheet and spread the above mixture evenly over the parchment. Cool for 1 hour or until set.
- Meanwhile, over medium low heat, melt together butter and semi-sweet chocolate chips.
- Spread chocolate sauce over the base, let set and cut into pieces of the size you desire.

Chewy Energy Bars

This chewy granola bar can be made with a variety of mixed dried fruits, nuts and seeds.

12 Servings	32 Servings	60 Servings	Ingredients
4 ½ cups	12 cups	22 cups	Mixed Dried Fruit (apricots, pitted dates, raisins and/or cranberries)
3 cups	8 cups	15 cups	Old Fashioned Rolled Oats
2 ¼ cups	6 cups	11 ¼ cups	Toasted Wheat Germ
2 cups	5 cups	10 cups	Honey or Brown sugar
1 ½ cups	4 cups	7 cups	Chopped Almonds, Walnuts or Pecans
1 cup	3 cups	8 cups	Pumpkin Seeds
½ cup	1 ½ cups	3 cups	Sesame seeds
1 tsp	2 tsp	1 Tbsp	Salt
1 Tbsp	8 Tbsp	15 Tbsp	Cinnamon
1 ½ cups	4 cups	7 cups	Coconut
1 cup	3 cups	5 ½ cups	Butter or non-hydrogenated Margarine
1 ½ cups	4 cups	7 cups	Corn Syrup or Brown Rice Syrup
1 Tbsp	3 Tbsp	8 Tbsp	Vanilla

Directions:

- Preheat oven to 350˚F and grease a large cookie sheet with Pam (or use a parchment).
- Dice dried fruit into small pieces. In a large bowl, combine dried fruit with the dry ingredients.
- Toast wheat germ in the oven for about 10 minutes.
- Over medium heat, melt butter or non-hydrogenated margarine and combine brown rice syrup or corn syrup with honey or sugar. Bring to a light boil and pour over the dry ingredients. Add vanilla and mix ingredients until blended well.
- Press mixture into pan and bake until golden brown.

Chewy Peanut Butter Energy Bars

A high protein snack, sure to make anyone shift gears. Try using any combination of ingredients such as miniature chocolate chips, sunflower seeds and other seeds, chopped dried fruits, and chopped nuts.

12 Servings	32 Servings	60 Servings	Ingredients
4 ½ cups	12 cups	22 cups	Mixed Dried Fruit (apricots, pitted dates, raisins and/or cranberries)
3 cups	8 cups	15 cups	Old Fashioned Rolled Oats
3 cups	8 cups	15 cups	Honey or Brown Rice Syrup
1 ½ cups	4 cups	7 cups	Chopped Almonds, Walnuts or Pecans
1 tsp	2 tsp	1 Tbsp	Salt
1 Tbsp	8 Tbsp	15 Tbsp	Cinnamon
1 ½ cups	4 cups	7 cups	Coconut
1 ½ cups	4 cups	7 cups	Chocolate Chips
1 ¼ cups	4 cups	7 cups	Butter, non-hydrogenated margarine, or apple sauce
2 1/2 cups	6 cups	11 1/4 cups	Peanut Butter
1 Tbsp	3 Tbsp	8 Tbsp	Vanilla

Directions:

- Preheat oven to 350°F and grease a large cookie sheet with Pam (or use a parchment).
- Combine dry ingredients in a bowl.
- In a large pot combine wet ingredients and stir until blended well.
- Combine with dry ingredients and press mixture into pan and bake until golden brown.

Apricot Granola Bars

For a healthier alternative to corn syrup try substituting brown rice syrup or honey.

12 Servings	32 Servings	60 Servings	Ingredients
¾ cup	2 cups	3 ¾ cups	Unsalted Butter
¾ cup	2 cups	3 ¾ cups	Liquid Honey
1 Tbsp	3 Tbsp	5 Tbsp	Vanilla
4 ½ cups	12 cups	22 ½ cups	Rolled Oats
1 ½ cup	4 cups	7 ½ cups	Slivered Almonds
1 ½ cup	4 cups	7 ½ cups	Salted Peanuts
1 ½ cup	4 cups	7 ½ cups	Flaked Coconut
9 Tbsp	1 ½ cups	3 cups	Corn Syrup, Honey or Brown Rice Syrup
1 ½ cups	4 cups	7 ½ cups	Dried Chopped Apricots
1 ½ cups	4 cups	7 ½ cups	Chocolate Chips

Directions:

- Preheat oven to 350°F.
- Melt butter and mix in honey and vanilla.
- Add nuts, fruit and oats to wet mixture. Add chocolate chips once mixture has cooled.
- Bake until golden brown.

Fruit & Seed Bars

A delicious and healthy snack for those on the go.

12 Servings	32 Servings	60 Servings	Ingredients
¾ cup	2 cups	3 ¾ cups	Unsalted Butter or non-hydrogenated Margarine
¾ cup	2 cups	3 ¾ cups	Liquid Honey
1 Tbsp	3 Tbsp	8 Tbsp	Vanilla
1 ½ cups	4 cups	7 cups	Sunflower Seeds
1 ½ cups	4 cups	7 cups	Pumpkin Seeds
1 ½ cups	4 cups	7 cups	Flax Seeds
1 ½ cups	4 cups	7 cups	Poppy Seeds
1 ½ cups	4 cups	7 cups	Rolled Oats
1 ½ cups	4 cups	7 cups	Dried Cranberries
1 ½ cups	4 cups	7 cups	Apricots
1 ½ cups	4 cups	7 cups	Dates
1 ½ cups	4 cups	7 cups	Frozen Orange Juice Concentrate

Directions:

- Preheat oven to 350°F. Melt butter or non-hydrogenated margarine and let cool slightly.
- Mix honey and vanilla with nuts, fruit and oats. Add thawed orange juice and butter. Bake until golden brown.

Vegan Granola Bars

Use carob chips as a dairy free option for these vegan granola bars.

12 Servings	32 Servings	60 Servings	Ingredients
1 ½ cup	4 cups	7 ½ cups	Brown Rice Syrup or Agave Syrup
1 ½ cup	4 cups	7 ½ cups	Melted Non-hydrogenated Margarine
2 cups	7 cups	12 cups	Peanut Butter or Almond Butter
1 Tbsp	3 Tbsp	5 Tbsp	Vanilla
9 cups	24 cups	45 cups	Quick Oats
1 ½ cups	4 cups	7 ½ cups	Sunflower Seeds
1 ½ cups	4 cups	7 ½ cups	Coconut
1 ½ cups	4 cups	7 ½ cups	Carob Chips

Directions:

- In a medium saucepan over medium low heat, melt non-hydrogenated margarine and combine peanut butter, brown rice syrup or agave syrup, vanilla and oats.
- Mix thoroughly and then blend in the coconut and sunflower seeds. Once the mixture has cooled, stir in the carob chips and press into a large greased or parchment-lined cookie sheet and let set for 1 hour.
- Cut into 4 inch squares.

Oatmeal Raspberry Bars

This yummy treat has a tender cookie bottom and is topped with a jam preserve. Try raspberry, strawberry or a mix of the two.

12 Servings	32 Servings	60 Servings	Ingredients
1 ½ cups	4 cups	15 cups	Butter or non-hydrogenated Margarine
1 ½ cups	4 cups	15 cups	Brown sugar
3 cups	8 cups	15 cups	Flour
¾ tsp	2 tsp	3 ¾ tsp	Baking Soda
¾ tsp	2 tsp	3 ¾ tsp	Salt
3 cups	8 cups	15 cups	Rolled Oats
2 ¼ cups	6 cups	11 ¼ cups	Raspberry Jam

Option: Sprinkle shredded coconut on top of raspberry jam instead of crumb mixture.

Directions:

- Mix together all of the ingredients except the raspberry or strawberry jam. Set aside ¼ of the mixture.
- Spread the mixture onto a parchment-lined cookie sheet, spread raspberry jam on top and sprinkle the remaining mixture on top of that. Bake at 350°F for 30 - 40 minutes.

Fudgy Chocolate Brownies

The key to great brownies is to undercook them a little bit in the center—even when they seem like they are underdone, pull them out. As the brownies cool they will set.

12 Servings	32 Servings	60 Servings	Ingredients
225 g	560 g	900 g	Semi-Sweet Chocolate ***or***
1 ½ cups	3 cups	5 cups	Fry's Cocoa
1 cup	2 ½ cups	4 cups	Butter or non-hydrogenated margarine
4 cups	10 cups	16 cups	Brown Sugar
8	20	32	Eggs
1 Tbsp	3 Tbsp	5 Tbsp	Vanilla
2 cups	5 cups	8 cups	Flour
2 cups	5 cups	8 cups	Pecans or walnuts/ dried cranberries/ dried cherries/chunky chocolate (optional)

Directions:

- Melt together chocolate and butter and let cool. It is important to let the chocolate cool before adding to the other ingredients, as otherwise it will cause your brownies to become dry and cakey.
- Combine sugar, eggs and vanilla. Add cooled chocolate mixture to sugar and eggs. Add flour to mixture. Mix with only a few swift strokes.
- Pour into a greased or parchment-lined 2 inch hotel pan (or a large cookie sheet for thinner brownies) and bake for 20 minutes at 350°F.
- Serve with whipped cream or ice cream.

Chocolate Chip Granola Spice Cookies

A delightfully spiced granola cookie with a hint of molasses.

12 Servings	32 Servings	60 Servings	Ingredients
3 cups	8 cups	15 cups	Butter or non-hydrogenated Margarine
1 ½ cups	4 cups	7 cups	Brown Sugar
6 Tbsp	1 cup	1 ½ cups	Molasses
3 cups	8 cups	15 cups	Sugar
3 ¾ cups	10 cups	18 ¼ cups	Flour
¾ cup	2 cups	3 ¾ cups	Wheat Germ
3 cups	8 cups	15 cup	Granola
3 cups	8 cups	15 cups	Chocolate Chips
4 ½ cups	12 cups	22 ½ cups	Rolled Oats
3	8	15	Eggs
1 ½ tsp	1 Tbsp	2 Tbsp	Cloves
1 Tbsp	2 ½ Tbsp	5 Tbsp	Baking Powder
1 Tbsp	2 ½ Tbsp	5 Tbsp	Allspice
1 Tbsp	2 ½ Tbsp	5 Tbsp	Nutmeg
1 Tbsp	2 ½ Tbsp	5 Tbsp	Baking Soda
1 Tbsp	2 ½ Tbsp	5 Tbsp	Vanilla

Directions:

- In a medium-sized bowl, measure margarine, brown sugar, molasses, vanilla and white sugar. Cream eggs with the above ingredients.
- Measure dry ingredients into a medium-sized bowl. Sift together and add chocolate chips.
- Slowly add dry ingredients to wet ingredients and mix well.
- Line a large cookie sheet with parchment and spread cookie dough over parchment.

Quick Tip: Chill dough before forming cookies for easier formation.

- Heat oven to 350°F and bake cookies for 30 minutes or until browned.

Hello Dollies

A decadent cookie bar that will leave you wanting more…

12 Servings	32 Servings	60 Servings	Ingredients
3 cups	8 cups	15 cups	Graham Wafer Crumbs
3 cups	8 cups	15 cups	Butter or non-hydrogenated Margarine
2 Tbsp	1 cup	1 ½ cups	Brown Sugar
3 300 ml cans	8 300 ml cans	10 300 ml cans	Sweet and Condensed Milk
6 cups	16 cups	30 cups	Coconut
4 ½ cups	12 cups	22 ½ cups	Chocolate Chips
3 cups	8 cups	15 cups	Pecans or Walnuts

Directions:

- Preheat oven to 350°F
- Melt non-hydrogenated margarine or butter in a sauce pan and, once it's melted, mix in graham crumbs and sugar.
- Press graham crumb mixture into a large cookie sheet.
- Spread sweet condensed milk over the graham crumb layer. Sprinkle with coconut, chocolate chips and walnuts or pecans.
- Drizzle the remaining sweet condensed milk over the chocolate and nuts and bake for 20-30 minutes.
- Let cool and slice into squares.
- ***Variation:*** Add minature marshmallows over the sweet and condensed milk and top with remaining ingredients.

Oatmeal Chocolate Cranberry Cookies

A pleasant mix of chocolate and dried cranberries makes this cookie an irresistible hit.

12 Servings	32 Servings	60 Servings	Ingredients
3 cups	8 cups	15 cups	Butter or non-hydro-genated Margarine
3 cups	8 cups	15 cups	Brown Sugar
1 Tbsp	3 Tbsp	5 Tbsp	Vanilla
6	16	30	Eggs
1 ½ Tsp	1 ½ Tbsp	2 Tbsp	Salt
1 Tbsp	2 ½ Tbsp	5 Tbsp	Baking Soda
1 Tbsp	2 ½ Tbsp	5 Tbsp	Baking Powder
7 ½ cups	20 cups	37 ½ cups	Rolled Oats
6 cups	16 cups	30 cups	Flour
6 cups	16 cups	30 cups	Chocolate chips
3 cups	8 cups	15 cups	Dried Cranberries

Directions:

- Preheat oven to 350°F.
- Measure dry ingredients into a large bowl. Measure the wet ingredients into another large bowl. Pour the dry ingredients into the wet ingredients and mix using your hands. Chill dough for 1 hour to make it easier to place on a cookie sheet.
- Using a large hotel sheet, place parchment over the cookie sheet and roll out dough over the sheet. Wet your hands in water to prevent the dough from sticking to your hands and push the dough out toward the edges.
- Bake for 40 minutes or until golden brown.

Texas Ranger Cookies

A hearty cookie with a generous Smarty surprise.

12 Servings	32 Servings	60 Servings	Ingredients
3 cups	8 cups	15 cups	Butter
9	18	45	Eggs
3 cups	16 cups	30 cups	Flour
3 cups	16 cups	30 cups	Brown Sugar
3 cups	16 cups	30 cups	Corn Flakes or Special K
3 cups	16 cups	30 cups	Oatmeal
1 Tbsp	3 Tbsp	5 Tbsp	Baking Powder
2 Tbsp	6 Tbsp	10 Tbsp	Baking Soda
2 ¼ tsp	2 Tbsp	3 ½ Tbsp	Salt
3 cups	8 cups	15 cups	Smarties
1 Tbsp	2 ½ Tbsp	5 Tbsp	Vanilla

Directions:

- Mix the dry ingredients together in a large bowl. Add Smarties.
- Cream together butter and sugar. Add eggs and vanilla and whisk together until eggs are mixed in.
- Mix dry ingredients into the wet ingredients. Use your hands to thoroughly mix together the wet and dry ingredients.
- Place parchment over a large hotel sheet and spread cookie dough evenly over the hotel sheet.
- Bake at 350°F for 40 minutes or until golden brown. Cool and cut into squares.

Sour Cream Streusel Coffee Cake

One of my personal favourites and great to have anytime of the day. The streusel topping is great to have on hand as it can be used for topping muffins too!

12 Servings	32 Servings	60 Servings	Ingredients
4 ½ cups	12 cups	22 ½ cups	All-purpose Flour
2 ¼ cups	6 cups	11 cups	Brown Sugar
¾ cup	2 cup	3 ¾ cups	Walnuts
1 Tbsp	2 Tbsp	5 Tbsp	Cinnamon
2 Tbsp	5 Tbsp	10 Tbsp	Baking Powder
1 ½ Tsp	2 ½ Tbsp	5 Tbsp	Baking Soda
¾ tsp	2 tsp	1 ¾ Tbsp	Salt
3 cups	8 cups	15 cups	Sour Cream
2 ¼ cups	6 cups	11 cups	Apple Sauce
6	16	30	Eggs

Streusel:

1 ½ cups	4 cups	7 cups	Brown Sugar
1 ½ cups	4 cups	7 cups	Flour
¾ cup	2 cups	4 cups	Butter
1 Tbsp	2 ½ Tbsp	5 Tbsp	Cinnamon

Directions:

- Preheat oven to 350°F
- In a large bowl, combine dry ingredients and set aside. Finely chop walnuts and add to dry ingredients.
- In another bowl combine sour cream, applesauce and eggs and whisk together until eggs are light and fluffy.
- Add dry ingredients to the wet and stir until just mixed, otherwise if you over mix the dough it will become tough.
- Pour into greased bundt pans and sprinkle streusel over top. Bake for about 40 minutes or until browned on top. Test doneness with a toothpick, if the toothpick comes out clean then the cake is done.

- Let cool slightly and then turn the Bundt pan upside down onto a plate to remove cake from pan. If the cake is not coming out easily then gently tap the top of the pan until the cake is removed from the pan. Slice into individual pieces.

Strawberry Shortcake

An easy alternative to the real thing.

12 Servings	32 Servings	60 Servings	Ingredients
6	15	24	Eggs
1 1/3 cups	3 1/3 cups	5 1/3 cups	Water
2 1/2 cups	6 1/4 cups	10 cups	Sugar
3 cups	7 1/2 cups	12 cups	Cake Flour
2 tsp	1 3/4 Tbsp	2 3/4 Tbsp	Baking Powder
1 tsp	2 1/2 tsp	1 1/4 Tbsp	Salt
1 Tbsp	3 Tbsp	5 Tbsp	Vanilla
1 80g package	3 80 g packages	5 80 g packages	Instant Whipped Topping
1/2 lb	1 1/2 lbs	2 1/2 lbs	Sliced Strawberries

Directions:

- Preheat oven to 350°F.
- Separate egg yolks and whites.
- Combine flour, baking powder and salt in a medium-sized bowl and mix together.
- In a large bowl, beat egg yolks and water until 5 times the original size. Add sugar and beat.
- Beat egg whites until light and fluffy. Fold into egg yolk mixture.
- Add to dry ingredients and mix well.
- Pour into a greased 2 inch hotel pan(s) and bake for one hour. Let cool and spread instant whipped topping or prepared whipped cream over the top.
- Place sliced strawberries on top.

Variation: Substitute vanilla for lemon or almond extract.

Magic Mocha Torte Cake

A moist and savoury cake with a hint of coffee.

12 Servings	32 Servings	60 Servings	Ingredients
2 1/2 cups	12 1/2 cups	20 cups	Flour
1 ½ tsp	2 1/2 Tbsp	4 Tbsp	Baking Soda
1/3 cup	1 2/3 cups	2 2/3 cups	Instant Coffee
1 1/3 cups	6 1/2 cups	10 1/2 cups	Water
3	15	24	Eggs
1 tsp	1 Tbsp	3 Tbsp	Vanilla
1 cup	5 cups	8 cups	Mayonnaise or Miracle Whip
3 squares or 112g	12 sq. or 345g	24 sq. or 675g	Unsweetened Chocolate
1 ½ cups	7 1/2 cups	12 cups	Sugar

Directions:

- Preheat oven to 350°F.
- Over medium low heat place chocolate squares into a double boiler (use a glass bowl or stainless steel bowl placed over a medium-sized stock pot one-quarter filled with water). Bring water to a boil and let the heat from the double boiler melt the chocolate. Stir the chocolate as it melt.
- In a large bowl, sift together flour and baking soda.
- Dissolve instant coffee in hot water.
- Beat together sugar, eggs and vanilla until light and fluffy.
- Blend in mayo and melted chocolate.
- Alternately add flour mixture and coffee to the wet ingredients and blend on low speed.
- Pour mixture into greased 2 inch hotel pans or place parchment into pan followed by the cake batter.
- Bake for 35 - 40 minutes and let cool for 1 hour before serving.

Chocolate Frosting

A versatile frosting for any occasion.

12 Servings	32 Servings	60 Servings	Ingredients
1/2 cup	2 cups	3 1/4 cups	Butter
1/2 cup	11/4 cups	2 cups	Cocoa ***or***
4 squares	16 squares	24 squares	Unsweetened Chocolate
1 ¾ cups	7 cups	13 cups	Icing Sugar
1/2 cup	2 cups	4 cups	Milk

Directions:

- In a large bowl, cream together butter, cocoa, icing sugar and milk. If using unsweetend chocolate, melt over a double broiler, let cool and add to above ingredients omitting the cocoa.
- Spread evenly over chocolate cake.
- Try adding mint extract or instant coffee for a different twist.

Berry Coulis

A delicious fresh touch to any cake!

12 Servings	32 Servings	60 Servings	Ingredients
6 cups	16 cups	30 cups	Raspberries, Blackberries or both
1 Tbsp	3 Tbsp	5 Tbsp	Sugar

Directions:

- In a large pan, bring berries and sugar to a light simmer, using a hand blender, purée the berries into a nice sauce.
- Let cool and place into a squeeze bottle. Serve over chocolate cake covered with a generous layer of chocolate icing.

Whole Wheat Carrot Cake

A creamy moist cake with a decadent cream cheese icing… suitable for all ages!

12 Servings	32 Servings	60 Servings	Ingredients
3 cups	7 1/2 cups	12 cups	Whole Wheat Flour
1 Tbsp	2 1/2 Tbsp	4 Tbsp	Baking Soda
2 tsp	1 ¼ Tbsp	2 ½ Tbsp	Baking Powder
2 Tsp	3 Tbsp	5 Tbsp	Cinnamon
1 Tsp	2 Tbsp	4 Tbsp	Allspice
1 Tsp	1 Tbsp	1 1/2 Tbsp	Nutmeg
1 Tsp	3/4 Tbsp	1 1/4 Tbsp	Salt
6	15	24	Eggs
2 cups	5 cups	8 cups	Brown Sugar
1 1/3 cups	3 1/3 cups	5 1/3 cups	Oil and/or Apple Sauce
1 Tbsp	3 Tbsp	5 Tbsp	Vanilla
3 cups	7 1/2 cups	12 cups	Grated Carrot
2 cups	5 cups	8 cups	Walnuts

Directions:

- Preheat oven to 350°F.
- Cream together eggs, sugar and oil and/or apple sauce. Add shredded carrots.
- Sift together flour, baking soda and powder, cinnamon, nutmeg, allspice and salt.
- Blend dry ingredients into wet ingredients.
- Pour into either a greased or parchment-lined 2 inch hotel pan and bake for 45 minutes or until golden brown on top.
- Test doneness with a toothpick.
- Let cool for 1 hour and ice with carrot cake icing.

Carrot Cake Icing

You can never make too much of this icing. If you have left over icing simply add some cocoa and use over any chocolate cake.

12 Servings	32 Servings	60 Servings	Ingredients
8 oz	16 oz	24 oz	Cream Cheese
2 cups	4 cups	6 cups	Icing Sugar
1/2 cup	1 cup	1 1/2 cups	Butter
1 Tbsp	2 Tbsp	3 Tbsp	Vanilla

Directions:

- Have all ingredients at room temperature.
- Using a handheld blender or stand mixer, beat ingredients until blended together.
- Frost carrot cake when cool.

Chocolate Chip Chocolate Zucchini Cake

For a lower fat cake try using apple sauce instead of oil, makes a great tasting cake!

12 Servings	32 Servings	60 Servings	Ingredients
1 ½ cups	5 cups	8 cups	Oil or Apple Sauce
3 cups	7 1/2 cups	12 cups	Sugar
1 ½ cups	2 1/2 cups	4 cups	Milk or Yogurt
2	5	8	Eggs
1 Tbsp	3 Tbsp	5 Tbsp	Vanilla
2 cups	5 cups	8 cups	Shredded Zucchini
6 cups	12 1/2 cups	20 cups	Flour
1 ½ cups	5 cups	8 cups	Cocoa
2 tsp	1 ½ Tbsp	2 Tbsp	Baking Soda
1 tsp	3/4 Tbsp	1 1/4 Tbsp	Baking Powder
1 tsp	3/4 Tbsp	1 1/4 Tbsp	Salt
1 tsp	1 Tbsp	1 1/2 Tbsp	Cinnamon
1/2 cup	1 1/2 cups	3 cups	Chocolate Chips

Directions:

- Preheat oven to 375 °F.
- Measure dry ingredients into a large bowl. Shred zucchini and set aside.
- Combine wet ingredients and whisk in eggs. Add shredded zuchinni. Add dry ingredients to the wet ingredients and mix using a wooden spoon.
- Place cake into a greased hotel pan(s) and bake for 40 minutes. Test for doneness by using a toothpick. Instead of greasing the pan you could use parchment paper to prevent the cake from sticking to the sides.
- Let cool, spread chocolate ganache icing over top and cut into ½ inch pieces.

Chocolate Ganache Icing

12 Servings	32 Servings	60 Servings	Ingredients
1 1/2 Cups	7 1/2 Cups	12 Cups	Semi Sweet Chocolate Chips
1/2 cup	2 1/2 cups	4 cups	Cream

Directions:

- Over a double boiler, in a glass bowl combine semi sweet chocolate chips and cream and melt chocolate until combined with the cream. Add more cream if you find the mixture to hard to spread.

Land of Nod Cinnamon Buns

So easy and great tasting… a definite pleaser!

12 Servings	32 Servings	60 Servings	Ingredients
1	2-3	3-4	Whole Wheat Frozen Dinner Rolls
1 ½ cup	3 cups	5 cups	Butter
1 80 g package	2 80 g packages	3 80 g packages	Vanilla Instant Pudding
1 ½ cups	4 cups	7 cups	Brown Sugar
½ cup	2 cups	4 cups	Cinnamon

Directions:

- Using a Bundt pan or a spring form pan, grease pan with some of the melted butter. Mix cinnamon and brown sugar together and sprinkle half the mixture on the bottom of the greased pan. Sprinkle with ¼ of the vanilla pudding powder. Add frozen dinner rolls to the pan and pour the remainder of the cinnamon, brown sugar and vanilla pudding powder over the buns. Pour the rest of the melted butter over the buns.
- Cover and let rise overnight in a warm area of the kitchen.
- Preheat oven to 375°F Bake in for 45 minutes or until golden brown on top. Place bundt pan upside down to remove the cinnamon buns from the pan.

Whole Wheat Banana Muffins

What would a cookbook be without banana muffins!

12 Servings	32 Servings	60 Servings	Ingredients
3 Cups	8 Cups	15 Cups	Ripe Banana
1 ½ Cups	4 Cups	7 Cups	Yogurt or Sour cream
6	16	30	Eggs
1 Tbsp	3 Tbsp	8 Tbsp	Vanilla
6 Cups	16 Cups	30 Cups	Whole Wheat Flour
3 Cups	8 Cups	15 Cups	Brown Sugar
1 Tbsp	3 Tbsp	5 Tbsp	Baking Powder
1 Tbsp	3 Tbsp	5 Tbsp	Baking Soda
1 Tbsp	3 Tbsp	5 Tbsp	Salt
2 ¼ Cup	6 Cups	11 ¼ Cups	Butter or oil
1 ½ Cups	4 Cups	7 Cups	Walnuts and/or Chocolate chips and/or Craisons

Directions:

- Preheat oven to 350°F.
- Combine wet ingredients and wisk until eggs are well blended.
- Peel bananas and mash. Add to wet ingredients.
- Combine dry ingredients in a large bowl.
- Wisk wet ingredients into the dry. Mix only until the wet and dry ingredients are just blended. Over mixing will cause the muffins to be dense and will not rise properly.
- Pour into greased muffin tins or loaf pans.
- Bake 25 – 30 minutes for muffins or 40 -50 minutes for loaf.

MEASUREMENT CONVERSIONS

A pinch/to taste/a dash = Less than 1/8 tsp

1/8 tsp = .5 ml

¼ tsp = 1.0 ml

½ tsp = 2.0 ml

¾ tsp = 4 ml

1tsp = 5 ml

1 ½ tsp = 7 ml

1 Tbsp = 15 ml

2 Tbsp = 25 ml

¼ cup = 50 ml

1/3 cup = 75 ml

½ cup = 125 ml

2/3 cup = 150 ml

¾ cup = 175 ml

3 tsp = 1 Tbsp

16 Tbsp = 1 cup

½ Tbsp = 1 ½ tsp

¼ cup = 4 Tbsp

1/3 cup = 5 1/3 Tbsp

½ cup = 8 Tbsp

2/3 cup = 10 2/3 Tbsp

¾ cup = 12 Tbsp

1 cup = 16 Tbsp = 250 ml

2 cups = 1 pint

4 cups = 1 quart

2 pints = 1 quart

4 quarts = 1 gallon

16 oz = 2 Cups = 480 ml

1 quart = 4 cups = 1 litre

¼ lb = 4 oz = 114 grams

½ lb = 16 oz = 454 grams

2 lbs = 907 grams

2.2 lbs = 1 kg

INDEX

C

D

E

F

N

O

P

As a way of giving back to all who have supported me in writing this cookbook, a portion of the proceeds from each cookbook sold will be donated to The Andean Research Institute…

The Andean Research Institute

Our vision is to keep the sacred wisdom of the Andes and the Amazon alive, and through embodying the wisdom, grow a conscious relationship with the land and model responsible ways of living on earth.
Our mission is to document this sacred wisdom, to support the keepers of the wisdom in their transition into a modern world, to provide social and economic outreach in their communities, and through land acquisition, preserve the fragile Amazon Rainforest.

The hub of our activities is located in the village of Maras, which sits above the Sacred Valley of the Inkas near Cusco. Our facility has living quarters for volunteers, a kitchen, bathrooms, meeting areas, and gardens. Water is very scarce in this area, and we'll be drilling our own water well as soon as possible. Our programs are growing rapidly, and we are currently fundraising for additional living quarters, meeting spaces, and land acquisition in the Amazon.

ARI originated in 1999 as part of the 'Giving Back' program at the Rainbow Jaguar Institute. Since then, ARI has had a continuous presence through different assistance projects. Our 'giving back' efforts are the source of the respect and recognition we receive from the villages and medicine people we serve.

At ARI, we focus our efforts in three areas;

• Inka Healing Technologies
The Inka are keepers of the rich millennia-old healing technology of mind, body, and spirit. Industrialization, social change, and current economies have threatened its survival and continuity. This ancient wisdom holds vital keys to social well-being, and it is imperative that we preserve it.

• Social Change and Empowerment
Peru is a third world country with abandoned populations scattered throughout its diverse landscapes. Historically, they have been ravaged by social and economical changes. Our focus is to provide communities with educational and economic opportunities.

• Rainforest Preservation
The Amazon Rainforest and its rich bio-diversity is under severe threat of a different order. Through land acquisition and preservation we are working to support the future of the human and ecological biodiversity of this region.

Judy, on behalf of the medicine people, the children, the communities that ARI supports, we thank you. We also extend our thanks to you – the buyer of this amazing cookbook.

For more information, please visit our website at www.andeaninstitute.org